USA TODAY'S DEBATE: VOICES AND PERSPECTIVES

ANIMAL RIGHTS

Noble Cause or Needless Effort?

Marna Owen

Twenty-First Century Books · Minneapolis

Twenty-First Century Books
A division of Lerner Publishing Group, Inc.
241 First Avenue North
Minneapolis, MN 55401 U.S.A.

Website address: www.lernerbooks.com

The publisher wishes to thank Ben Nussbaum and Phil Pruitt of USA TODAY for their help in preparing this book.

Library of Congress Cataloging-in-Publication Data

Owen, Marna A.
    Animal rights : noble cause or needless effort? / by Marna Owen.
        p.   cm. — (USA TODAYS's debate : voices and perspectives)
    Includes bibliographical references and index.
    ISBN 978-0-7613-4082-9 (lib. bdg. : alk. paper)
    1. Animal rights. 2. Animal welfare. I. Title.
    HV4708.O838 2010
    179'.3—dc22   2009004813

Manufactured in the United States of America
1 2 3 4 5 6 – DP – 15 14 13 12 11 10

CONTENTS

Introduction

THE TEMPERATURE WAS APPROACHING 100°F (38°C) on the afternoon of August 28, 2006, in Chandler, Arizona. But the scorching weather didn't stop about thirty people from taking to the streets in response to Covance Laboratories' plans to construct a new testing facility in Chandler.

Covance is one of the world's largest pharmaceutical companies. The company has helped develop and test the safety of many of the drugs that are currently on the market, including lifesaving medications for controlling diseases such as diabetes and cancer. The new facility in Chandler would offer Covance easy access to other pharmaceutical and biotechnology (the use of microscopic organisms to perform industrial functions such as drug creation) facilities in the western United States. Meanwhile, the nearby University of Arizona and Arizona State University would provide researchers and scientists who could work in the company's labs.

Left: Residents of Chandler, Arizona, protest the expansion of a Covance laboratory in their city. The protesters object to Covance's use of animals in its research.

But on that hot day in August, students from nearby Arizona State University, among others, were standing on the street in protest of the new testing facility. Why? According to the protesters, Covance is well known for its use of laboratory animals in research and testing. The protesters, holding signs that said, "Covance Killed Beagles in Tobacco Tests," didn't want Covance testing drugs on animals in Chandler—or anywhere.

THE OTHER VIEWPOINT

Covance does not deny testing on animals. The company claims that animal testing is needed to ensure the safety of the drugs that will be put on the market for humans. The company says it follows a strict code of conduct when dealing with its test animals. The code, company officials said, ensures the comfort and humane treatment of test animals at all times. Covance's code—similar to that of many testing facilities around the world—is as follows:

1. We will treat animals in our care with respect. We honor the contribution that animals in our care make to lifesaving advances and will treat these animals with the respect that they deserve.
2. We will strictly follow all applicable laws and regulations for animal treatment.
3. We will employ alternative scientific methods to animal use where appropriate under applicable regulation and scientific validity.
4. We will minimize animal discomfort. We will work, consistent with the study protocol [guidelines] and good science, to reduce discomfort or stress to animals in our care.
5. We will take steps to ensure that our employees and processes meet these standards. We will train Covance employees who handle animals on proper procedures and techniques and will apply appropriate controls to ensure that these procedures

and techniques and this Code of Respect are followed. We will encourage employees to report any misconduct or failure to adhere to this Code of Respect.

6. If we learn that we or any of our employees have failed to follow this Code of Respect, we will take appropriate remedial [corrective] and disciplinary action.

In addition to developing lifesaving drugs for humans, Covance promised to greatly strengthen the city's economy. It would add about seven hundred jobs for residents of Chandler and the surrounding cities and would contribute millions of dollars to the city's economy.

Arizona State University student Jeff Lowe attended the protest in Chandler that day. But Lowe, along with a small handful of others, wasn't protesting Covance. He was there to speak out against the animal rights protesters. Lowe worked for a laboratory in high school and participated in testing on rats. Lowe said that the animals in the lab were always treated humanely. For him, the knowledge that he and other students gained from the research was well worth the deaths of the rats in the experiments. Lowe, too, held a picket sign. His stated, "Human Life Is Greater Than Animal Life." Lowe's argument was that Covance would be a boon to Chandler's economy and to the pharmaceutical industry as a whole.

Overall, most people in the Chandler area seemed to agree with Lowe. A public opinion poll in Chandler found that 62 percent of people favored construction of the new facility. Supporters of the Covance facility looked forward to the boost in their economy that would come from the new facility.

THE CONTROVERSY

The Covance incident shows two sides of a complicated debate, one that goes far beyond the use of animals in medical research. It is a controversy that raises many questions about how humans use and treat animals in daily life.

For example, should humans eat meat? Many animal rights groups believe that humans systematically and brutally murder billions of cows, pigs, and chickens each year for food. While some animal rights supporters argue for strict vegetarianism (meatless diets), other supporters favor laws that enforce painless methods of butchering animals.

Others reply that by eating meat, humans are simply carrying out their natural role in the food chain. Animals eat plants or other animals, and so do humans. The thought of an owl eating a mouse, for example, seems natural to most people. Is the idea of a person eating meat different somehow?

The animal rights debate stretches far beyond medical science and food. For example, should people use animals to make clothing, furniture, and other useful, everyday products? The practice dates back to the earliest humans, who used the skins and bones of other species for clothing and tools. Some animal rights advocates argue that in prehistoric times, animal parts were the sole available material for producing items such as clothing. In modern times, they say, technology has provided the means to produce synthetic (artificial) materials that can be used in place of animal skins. Other people argue that nothing matches the beauty, quality, and durability of products made from natural skins. They also point out that many synthetic materials are made from chemical processes that pollute the environment. And many of these synthetics are made from petroleum by-products and other mineral resources that are not renewable.

Should humans keep other animal species as pets, or is the very word *pet* demeaning? Some activists favor the term *companion animal* and believe that house animals deserve the same treatment as family members and friends. Some people firmly believe that animals are not meant to be kept indoors or in captivity (in zoos and aquariums, for example). Furthermore, where should humans draw the line on the

Above: A woman takes her dog for a walk. Some animal rights activists question whether humans should keep any animals as pets.

negatively to the extreme, sometimes illegal, tactics used by some activists in their attempt to gain and protect the rights of animals. Many people seek a middle ground that protects animals but allows them to be used, without cruelty, for specific purposes, such as for food, clothing, and medical research.

What guidelines should be in place concerning human relationships with and responsibilities toward animals? At the heart of the animal rights debate are these questions: Do all animals have rights just as humans do? Do animals deserve the same treatment as humans? Do humans have the right to use other species for their own purposes? Is there some middle ground on which the two sides can agree?

type of animals kept as pets? If cats and dogs are acceptable pets, are tigers and other wild cats? What about wild dogs or wolves and exotic pets such as snakes, lizards, and monkeys?

Few people advocate cruelty to animals. But many of these same people may wonder why they should be as concerned about animals as they are about human beings. Many react

The animal rights debate is complicated and often filled with emotion. Issues are rarely black and white. With so complex an issue, almost as many different opinions exist as there are people.

CHAPTER ONE

History and Modern Thought

BASICALLY, TO HAVE A RIGHT IS TO HAVE A CLAIM OR entitlement to something and to have that claim recognized by others. In all societies, humans are believed to have certain rights—both legal (such as the right to vote) and moral. Moral rights, often called human rights, are more difficult to define than legal rights. They include such entitlements as "life, liberty, and the pursuit of happiness," as referred to in the Declaration of Independence adopted by the thirteen American colonies in 1776.

Humans believe that their moral rights stem from such qualities as reason, language, sentience (the ability to feel), self-awareness, forethought, intrinsic value (worth), and a sense of personal identity. Should rights for animals be based on the same criteria? If so, how do we determine whether animals possess these qualities?

Left: This section of Italian painter Raphael's *The School of Athens* shows Greek philosophers Plato *(center left)* and Aristotle *(center right)* talking in a Greek meeting place. The artwork was painted in the early sixteenth century. Aristotle believed that a human being's ability to reason gave humans power over animals.

For thousands of years, philosophers have wrestled with the question of animal rights: Do animals have rights? Are humans superior to other animals on Earth? Can animals reason, feel, and communicate?

AN ANCIENT DEBATE

Hinduism, the major religion of India, is one of the oldest religions in the world. Its roots reach back to prehistoric times. According to Hindu beliefs, animals have immortal (undying) souls just as human beings do. Hindus believe that the souls of animals are no different from the souls of human beings. As such, Hindus revere many animals. Among Hinduism's sacred animals are cows, monkeys, and snakes. Hinduism teaches that the soul never dies. When the body dies, the soul is reborn. In this continuous process of rebirth, called reincarnation, the soul can be reborn in an animal or in a human. Because Hindus view animals as sacred beings, most Hindus practice vegetarianism.

Ancient Jews had a slightly different view of the treatment of animals. They accepted a natural order in which one animal

Below: Hindus—who practice vegetarianism—consider cows sacred. This Hindu boy is worshipping a decorated cow on the streets of Allahabad, India.

Bulls and Bears

The ancient Romans had little regard for the lives and welfare of animals. Animals were routinely slain for entertainment. One particularly cruel act common in Rome was to chain two animals together—usually a bull and a bear—and force them to battle to the death. Criminals and non-Roman citizens were often given the status of animals as well. They could also be chained to a wild beast and forced to fight to the death.

(or person) would kill another for food. They thought of the act as a necessary evil. As a result, they offered their domestic animals basic protection from cruelty and did not kill wild animals indiscriminately. They believed that in heaven, the predator-prey relationship would be eliminated.

European societies, on the other hand, have long believed in human superiority over animals. For example, the ancient Greek philosopher Aristotle (384–322 B.C.) saw humans as rational beings capable of reason. Because humans can reason, Aristotle thought they rightly had dominion, or power, over plants and animals. He wrote that in the natural order of things, plants live to provide food for animals. In turn, animals live to supply humans with food, clothing, and tools. According to Aristotle, by using and consuming animals, humans are fulfilling their part in the natural hierarchy of life on Earth. It is worth noting, however, that Aristotle did not view all human beings as equals. Slaves, he believed, existed to serve their masters, much in the way he thought animals existed to serve humans.

IMPACT OF CHRISTIANITY

Christianity, the religion of much of Europe and the Americas, is rooted in the belief that humans are superior to animals.

The story of creation puts forth a clear statement about the relationship between humans and other animals. In the book of Genesis 1:26, the Bible states:

> And God said, Let us make man in our image, after our likeness: and let them have dominion over the fish of the sea, and over the fowl of the air, and over the earth, and over every creeping thing that creepeth upon the earth.

In this way, the Bible does not afford equal rights to animals. It implies that humans are superior beings with a special position in the universe because they resemble God. The words in Genesis also say that humans have dominion over everything else on Earth. Many people interpret this passage as God granting permission for humans to use animals as they wish.

Christian doctrine also states that humans are the only animals with immortal souls—the opportunity for spiritual life after bodily death. This doctrine has been held as truth for many centuries. So, according to many Christians, when animals die, they simply die. When people die, they experience life after death.

Italian Catholic priest and philosopher Thomas Aquinas lived in the 1200s. He summarized the common opinion of Christianity at the time, writing:

> We refute [do not accept] the error of those who claim that it is a sin for man to kill brute animals. For animals are ordered to Man's use in the natural course of things, according to divine providence [will]. Consequently, man uses them without any injustice, either by killing them or employing them in any other way.

Aquinas went on to state that animals lack intellect and therefore do not have a soul. Without a soul, he contended, animals do not have rights. He tempered his statement, however, saying that human beings should be sympathetic toward animals. He added this not because he thought that animals had any rights, however, but because he thought it was a good exercise in compassion. In other words, he believed that any kindness to animals should be done for the sake of strengthening human morals, not for the sake of the animals.

From the 1600s through the 1800s, a period called the Enlightenment, or the Age of Reason, European philosophers emphasized the use of reason as the best method of gaining truth. They believed that human beings had a unique advantage over all other creatures because humans can reason. Animals, in contrast, were thought to be slaves of their emotions. When an animal is threatened, it fights. When an animal is hungry, it will often attack other animals to lay claim to any nearby food. People, the philosophers argued, could solve their problems through reason. In the above examples, then, people might have a discussion to work through their anger. Or they might split the available food instead of fighting over it. Philosophers of the Enlightenment also noted that people, unlike animals, have a rational will (the ability to consciously make and carry out plans).

René Descartes, a seventeenth-century French philosopher, mathematician, and scientist, is called the father of

Above: René Descartes was an influential French thinker who lived in the seventeeth century. He believed that humans are superior to all other living things.

modern philosophy. Descartes was a Christian who believed that because humans have immortal souls and a mind with which to reason, they are superior to all other living things. He believed that only humans have

actively investigated anatomy (the study of the body). To learn how blood flows, scientists of the time nailed the paws of live dogs to boards and cut the dogs open. This procedure of live dissection is called vivisection.

> **" I believe I am not interested to know whether vivisection produces results that are profitable to the human race or doesn't. To know that the results are profitable to the race would not remove my hostility towards it. "**
>
> —**U.S. WRITER MARK TWAIN,**
> ON HIS VIEWS OF VIVISECTION, 1900

consciousness—shown by their unique capacity for language. Descartes believed that animals do not have minds, souls, or consciousness. Animals, in his view, are little more than machines, incapable of feeling.

EVOLVING ATTITUDES

During the 1600s and 1700s, scientific reasoning and experimentation advanced. For example, doctors and scientists

Anesthesia (drugs that lead to a loss of sensation, often by inducing a state of unconsciousness) did not exist at that time. All the same, experimenting on live animals without anesthesia seems cruel in modern times. Yet through these experiments, scientists were able to see how closely the bodies of animals resemble the bodies of humans. This resemblance helped reshape human attitudes toward

Above: A seventeenth-century European physician uses vivisection to demonstrate his theory of circulation of the blood.

animals and led to more humane treatment of them. For example, in the middle of the eighteenth century, the French author and philosopher François-Marie Arouet, better known by his pen name, Voltaire, referred to the "barbarous custom of supporting ourselves upon the flesh and blood of beings like ourselves." (Despite this view, Voltaire himself continued to eat meat.)

Even though European attitudes toward animals were changing as a result of scientific learning, many people held on to established views. For example, in 1789 the German philosopher

Immanuel Kant told his students that "so far as animals are concerned, we have no direct duties. Animals are not self-conscious, and are there merely as a means to an end. That end is man." Kant believed that the life of every human being had intrinsic worth and that only humans had an actual right to life.

At about the same time that Kant was lecturing, British philosopher Jeremy Bentham began to promote the idea of animal welfare. Questioning theories about the difference between humans and animals, he wrote:

> Is it the faculty of reason, or perhaps the faculty of discourse [talk, which distinguishes humans from animals]? But a full-grown horse or dog is beyond comparison a more rational, as well as a more conversable [communicative] animal, than an

Above: German philosopher Immanuel Kant *(left)* believed animals lacked self-consciousness, while British philosopher Jeremy Bentham *(right)* believed animals can suffer just as humans can.

infant of a day or week or even a month old. But suppose it were otherwise, what would it avail [matter]? The question is not, Can they *reason*? nor Can they *talk*? but, Can they suffer?

Bentham believed that in deciding what is right and wrong, the suffering of *all* creatures—not just that of humans—should be taken into account. In his view, just because an animal may not have the intellect of a human being does not mean the animal does not feel pain.

Science also changed the way people thought about the relationship between human beings and animals. Charles Darwin, a British naturalist of the nineteenth century, put forth a theory that revolutionized the way humans looked at their place in the natural world. In 1859 Darwin published *On the Origin of Species*.

In this book, Darwin proposed that one animal species could derive, or evolve, from another. Humans, however, were not yet included in Darwin's theory of evolution.

By 1871 many scientists had accepted Darwin's theory. In that year, he published *The Descent of Man*, a book that included humans in the evolutionary chain, stating that humans had

Above: Charles Darwin's books on evolution, published between 1850 and 1880, challenged the way most people saw the relationship between humans and animals.

evolved from other primates, such as apes and monkeys. Comparing the mental powers of humans and animals, he wrote:

> We have seen that the senses and intuitions, the various emotions and faculties, such as love, memory, attention and curiosity, imitation, reason, etc., of which man boasts, may be found in an incipient [undeveloped or emerging], or even sometimes in a well-developed condition, in the lower animals.

Darwin went on to say that the human moral sense could be traced back to social instincts in animals. These instincts, he claimed, led animals to take pleasure in each other's company, feel sympathy for each other, and mutually assist each other.

Darwin's book was extremely controversial, because it challenged the traditional understanding of the relationship between humans and animals. His theory contradicted Christian thinking on the subject, in which humans are viewed as superior to animals—and as a special creation of God. Many people of the time did not want to think of themselves as being part of the animal world. Nor did they feel comfortable with the challenge to the biblical time line of creation, in which humans are created in one instant, rather than evolving slowly over time. In the twenty-first century, many religious groups still disagree with and bitterly resent Darwin's theory that humans evolved from animals over time, even though the theory is generally accepted by the international scientific community.

A NEW UNDERSTANDING

Historically speaking, the debate over animal welfare is new. The American Society for the Prevention of Cruelty to Animals (ASPCA) formed in 1866. (Great Britain's Royal Society for the Prevention of Cruelty to Animals preceded it by twenty-six years.) The animal rights group known as People for the Ethical Treatment of Animals (PETA) followed more than one hundred years later, in 1980. Groups

Animal Rights vs. Animal Welfare

The terms *animal rights* and *animal welfare* are often used inter-changeably. But they don't mean the same thing. Animal rights imply that animals have a moral right to certain things, such as life and the prevention of cruelty. Animal welfare does not refer to rights but rather to the sense that animals should be treated with kindness and compassion.

such as these have made animal rights a national debate.

Scientific and medical knowledge has exploded over the past one hundred years, and much of that knowledge has come at the expense of animal lives and animal suffering. Countless vaccines, painkillers, and other medicines have been developed to give human beings longer, healthier lives. And many of these same medicines have also improved the lives of animals. But what of the cost?

Most animal rights supporters of the twenty-first century believe that animals experience a range of emotions that extends beyond primal feelings such as fear and aggression. Popular books, television programs, and scientific documentaries illustrate this point in various ways. For example, case studies indicate that rescue dogs suffer from depression resulting from their stressful work. Elephants exhibit an amazing level of patience with their young.

Scientists with firsthand knowledge of animals cite examples of animal behavior that seem to indicate the scope of animal emotion. For example, world-renowned scientist Jane Goodall is an expert in primate behavior. She spent many years in Africa studying chimpanzees and baboons. Goodall claims that chimps not only feel a wide range of emotions, but they also exhibit emotional behavior as humans do, including kissing, hugging, touching hands, patting on the back, and even tickling.

Animal rights supporters also cite studies that show how animals use language. In the 1960s and 1970s, for example, scientists taught a number of primates to use sign language. While many of the animals could use signs only to ask for simple things such as food and water, some could also combine signs in ways their teachers never showed them. One famous chimp named Lucy called a watermelon a "candy drink," and a radish a "hurt-cry food." A gorilla named Koko asked for a pet kitten and signed her sadness when it died. In addition, Goodall states that chimps in captivity can be taught more than three hundred signs.

Above: Jane Goodall observes two chimpanzees in Tanzania in 2006. Goodall has spent many years documenting primate behavior and believes chimps have a large capacity for sign language.

Other studies claim that some seals, sea lions, dolphins, and whales can apply grammatical rules to language. For example, dolphins at the Kewalo Basin Marine Mammal Laboratory in Honolulu, Hawaii, have been taught to understand about fifty words. The animals can carry out thousands of commands using only those fifty words. They understand the difference between "to left Frisbee, right surfboard take," and "to right surfboard, left Frisbee take." These sentences use the exact same words but have totally different meanings.

In 2006 another group of scientists used a computer program to analyze whale songs. The researchers found that whales communicated with one another in a way that was structurally similar to human speech. In other words, the researchers said that whales use bits of song to make up phrases of larger meaning, just as humans use words to make up sentences.

If that's not enough, some animals have even talked back.

An African Grey parrot named Alex showed scientists how advanced a bird's mind could be. Alex could count to six, identify colors and shapes, and even express his desires and frustrations. Alex, like many parrots, had the ability to mimic human sounds. He could use words and sentences in ways that suggested to researchers that he understood their meanings. Alex died in 2007 at the age of thirty.

Through studies such as these, researchers are finding that animals' understanding of and participation in language may indicate that they have higher reasoning abilities than was previously assumed. Maybe, as some animal rights supporters argue, animals are not incapable of communicating—they simply communicate in ways that humans can't easily understand. The idea that animals are able to use language only further blurs the line that separates them from people.

THE DEBATE CONTINUES

Other scientists and philosophers, however, say that recent experiments prove only that some creatures, indeed very few, can follow directions and have only limited capacity for language. They point out that dolphins do not write books nor do chimpanzees build rockets to the moon. They also argue that animals are not necessarily experiencing emotions as humans do. Rather humans are projecting emotions onto animals. This is a practice called anthropomorphism, or attaching human characteristics to animals or objects. For example, when a person looks into a puppy's soft, brown eyes, we may think we see sadness or longing, but do we assume the puppy feels these emotions only because we ourselves feel these emotions? Are humans projecting these emotions onto the puppy, or does the puppy really feel the same sorts of things humans do?

Many believe humans are the only beings capable of such emotions. Does this notion then mean that humans can treat animals any way they want? Peter Singer, director of the Centre for Human Bioethics at Monash University, in Australia, and the author of *Animal Liberation*, claims that because animals are sentient, the pain of a rat or a mouse or a dog is as important as the pain of a human. It is because animals are sentient, says Singer, that they deserve the same consideration given to humans. According to Singer, people who do not give equal consideration to animals make the same mistake as people who are racist or sexist. He calls these people speciesists.

However, Singer points out that equal consideration for animals does not necessarily lead to equal rights and equal treatment. "There are important differences between humans and other animals," he explains, "and these differences must give rise to some differences in the rights that each have."

When considering animal rights, Singer says, people ought to think in terms of doing the greatest good for the greatest number of living things. He believes humans must weigh whether the good gained by using animals for certain purposes exceeds the harm done to them. Does the welfare of all outweigh the suffering of a few? Is a cure for cancer worth the lives of experimental animals?

Above: Peter Singer's understanding of the value of life depends not on the species to which a living being belongs but upon the animal's ability to feel pain and pleasure.

U.S. philosopher and author Tom Regan rejects Singer's argument, which allows individual animals or humans to suffer if their suffering will benefit a great number of other humans or animals. Regan believes that all organisms have inherent value. Any organism that has beliefs, desires, perception, memory, a sense of the future, and a sense of identity over time and that can be benefited or harmed ought to be treated in ways that respect its value. According to Regan, humans fail to respect the inherent value of creatures when we do anything that harms them.

PETA takes that philosophy a step further. This national, nonprofit animal protection organization was founded by Alex Pacheco and Ingrid Newkirk. Its 1.8 million members are dedicated to establishing what they perceive as the rights of animals. Newkirk is often quoted as saying, "When it comes to feelings like pain, hunger, and thirst, a rat is a pig is a dog is a boy." Or the feelings of an animal aren't any less real than the feelings of a human.

Newkirk's view is shared by a growing number of animal rights activists who believe that animals should not be used for food, clothing, or medical research. Modern technology, they argue, offers many more humane alternatives to using animals. But that very same quote is used by people who

> " **Truthfully, animal-rightists have the public believing scientists can't wait to go to their labs every morning and torture animals. And that's the furthest case from the truth.** "
>
> —RICHARD TRAYSTMAN, HEAD OF THE ANIMAL WELFARE COMMITTEE AT JOHNS HOPKINS UNIVERSITY IN BALTIMORE, MARYLAND
>
> USA TODAY · OCTOBER 31, 2000

stand against animal rights. They claim that it shows that animal rights activists don't value the lives of human beings enough.

In recent years, the animal rights debate has given rise to extremist groups, whose members believe that animal rights must be achieved at any cost. A few of these groups are willing to use force, including violence against people, to gain rights for animals. These groups bring up a further question for animal rights supporters: if animals deserve more rights, is the fight to secure rights for *all* animals worth the lives of *some* humans?

MODERN THOUGHT

Opinion about the rights of animals still covers a wide spectrum. But opinions can generally be divided into three basic positions:

1. Humans are superior to animals. Animals are essentially our property, and we can use them as we please.
2. Animals should be used only in ways that greatly benefit humankind. Whenever possible, these animals should be treated without cruelty.
3. Animals have basic rights just as humans do. Animals should be allowed to live their lives naturally and without cruelty. Humans do not have the right to dominate or exploit animals for any reason.

People who hold the first position believe that humans have dominion over animals. Many of these people scoff at the idea of giving animals rights. Rights, they say, by their very definition, are restricted to human beings. Some people point to the food chain as evidence of human dominion over animals: humans eat animals, animals eat plants, and plants grow from decayed human and animal matter. To others, the idea of putting humans and pigs on equal footing seems absurd. For them, the suffering of a person with cancer or another disease will always be more important than the suffering of a laboratory rat.

www.usatoday.com

USA TODAY

Life
SECTION D

May 3, 2007

Britain Battles Animal Rights Radicals

From the Pages of
USA TODAY

LONDON—Animal-loving Britain, a hotbed of animal rights extremists, is saying "enough."

On Tuesday, British police launched the nation's biggest operation against animal rights militants. Thirty-two people were arrested in a coordinated morning sweep carried out by more than 700 officers across Britain and in Belgium and the Netherlands.

Those arrested are suspected of burglary, blackmail and acts of criminal intimidation against people working at or associated with university and bio-tech labs in Britain, police said.

The sweep came amid signs of a growing backlash against animal rights extremists, blamed for arson, beatings and vandalism at labs and businesses.

"Animal rights extremists have conducted sustained campaigns of harassment and intimidation against the animal research industry, seeking to achieve their objectives by creating a climate of fear," says Adrian Leppard, assistant chief constable of the Kent Police, which helped coordinate the raids Tuesday.

The raids follow a shift in public opinion on this side of the Atlantic, where animal welfare has roots in the early 19th century and where animal rights activism and violence are more common than in the USA.

There's growing acceptance of the need for animal testing for medical research, says John Leaman, a research director in London for the Ipsos MORI polling firm. "People have become weary of these extremist activities and tactics," he says.

The French love foie gras—goose and duck liver from birds that are force-fed to fatten them—producing and consuming 90% of the world's supply. Several European nations, including Denmark, Germany, Italy and Britain, ban its production as inhumane.

Britain banned fox hunting in 2004, and Queen Elizabeth faced public criticism in 2000 after she was photographed wringing the neck of a pheasant shot during a hunt. Britain has been home to large demonstrations against the use of animals in research.

Militants in Britain have targeted drug-company executives and others for attacks and intimidation:

- In 2001, the director of Europe's largest animal-testing lab, Huntingdon Life Sciences near Cambridge, was assaulted by men with ax handles.
- In 2005, the home of an executive at pharmaceutical firm GlaxoSmithKline was firebombed.
- Last year, activists threatened to publish the names of GlaxoSmithKline shareholders unless they sold their stock in the company.

Frankie Trull of the Washington-based National Association for Biomedical Research, which advocates the use of animals in research, says British activists share their tactics. "A lot of activists here (in the USA) go over there for training," she says.

Last year, President Bush signed legislation—the Animal Enterprise Terrorism Act—making it a crime to use force, violence or threats against companies engaged in animal research.

In Britain, the debate about extremists' tactics intensified in January when 16-year-old Laurie Pycroft encountered animal rights activists trying to block construction of a $35 million biomedical research lab. He and a friend marched in favor of the lab and drew support from Oxford University students, who formed the group Pro-Test in favor of animal testing.

Public opinion toward the use of animals in research was shifting here before last year.

In an Ipsos MORI Poll in December 2005, 75% of Britons said they condoned animal experiments for medical purposes. Fifty-two percent said they trusted scientists not to cause unnecessary suffering to lab animals, compared with 39% in 2002.

Activists "really do feel backed into a corner by a government" that allows vivisection of animals for research and wants to criminalize peaceful animal rights activities, Joshipura says. "There's a serious attempt . . . to silence the protesters."

Leppard, the Kent police official whose two-year investigation resulted in Tuesday's arrests, says police target only lawbreakers.

"The operation is not targeting lawful animal-welfare campaigners who have every right to express their personal views on such issues," he says.

—Jeffrey Stinson

The second position includes a wide range of middle ground. People who hold this position, which includes many animal welfare groups, believe humans have a responsibility to treat animals with kindness. It is acceptable to use animals to accomplish goals that will benefit society, as long as those goals are met through the kindest way possible. People holding this position may accept that humans have dominion over animals, but they don't believe this dominion includes the right to treat animals with cruelty.

This position—the belief that animals should be treated humanely—is probably the most common view in the twenty-first century. Most people in this category believe animals should be treated humanely and without cruelty, but not at the cost of human well-being. The bottom line for the majority of people who subscribe to the animal welfare position is that animals

Because of their proximity to the animals, ranchers *(below)* and farmers often feel differently about animals than do people who live in cities.

are important, but humans come first.

The third position states that animals should have all the rights of humans. Those who subscribe to this position see no significant differences between humans and animals. They believe that animals deserve treatment equal to that of human beings and that it is wrong for human beings to use animals in research and industry. They would like humans to allow animals to live their lives without interference from humans.

Although opinion about the relationship between humans and animals has changed over the centuries, many questions remain unanswered. Attitudes about animals are influenced by many factors, such as religious beliefs, where a person lives, and the kind of work they do. Ranchers in the Southwest, for example, may view cattle quite differently than do people who live in cities, where they may never encounter a cow except as packaged meat. To some people, pets are a messy nuisance. Others treat them as human beings. A medical researcher may view rats as a means to cure disease. Animal rights activists view the researcher's rats as helpless victims. Sometimes these philosophies clash.

CHAPTER TWO

Animals and the Law

IN 1821 ALDERMAN C. SMITH SUGGESTED TO THE British Parliament (lawmaking body) that a law should be passed protecting horses from cruel treatment. The other members of Parliament snickered, shouting that soon they'd be forced to protect dogs and cats. Soon the whole building shook with laughter at the thought. Protection for animals indeed! The notion was considered hilarious.

Since then attitudes about laws for the protection of animals have changed. Almost 170 years after the uproar in the British Parliament, the international peacekeeping organization known as the United Nations (UN) adopted a resolution calling for an end to all large-scale drift-net fishing. The resolution, most recently updated in 2002, targets the fishing fleets of Japan, Taiwan, and Korea. Fishing boats from these nations often use drift nets, which are sometimes 50 miles (80 kilometers) long. Drift nets are used mainly

Left: A dolphin is caught in a drift net. Many countries and international organizations are working to outlaw drift-net fishing because animals not meant to be trapped frequently end up being caught.

to catch tuna, but dolphins, sea turtles, seals, and many other creatures become tangled and are killed in them as well. Before the resolution, half a million seabirds died in the nets every year. Many of the animals that were caught could not be sold, so they were thrown away. The UN resolution was passed to help stop the waste and to protect animal life.

This example shows how far animal protection laws have come. Once scoffed at, animal protection has become an international issue. While some groups say the laws still need to be strengthened, others argue that the laws have already gone too far.

LAWS FOR HUMANE SLAUGHTER

Laws for animal welfare have been around for a long time. And as technologies change over time, so do the laws. The body of laws regulating the slaughter of animals for food is an excellent case example.

Before the 1800s, the treatment of animals that were to be slaughtered for their meat got little consideration. That changed in 1822, when the British Parliament passed a bill that made the mistreatment of certain animals an offense. It was the first law of its kind, and it was very controversial. Under the new law, animals were viewed as property, not as beings worthy of rights. And the law applied to farm animals such as cattle, horses, and donkeys—not to dogs and cats.

To enforce the new law, Richard Martin, a member of the British Parliament, and a group of other humanitarians formed the Royal Society for the Prevention of Cruelty to Animals (RSPCA) in 1824. The RSPCA formed a committee that inspected slaughterhouses, markets, and other places where animals were kept or used for work. A few years later, the RSPCA began employing formal inspectors to enforce the law. Then, in 1866, Henry Bergh, a New York philanthropist, founded a similar organization, the American Society for the Prevention of Cruelty to Animals, in the United States.

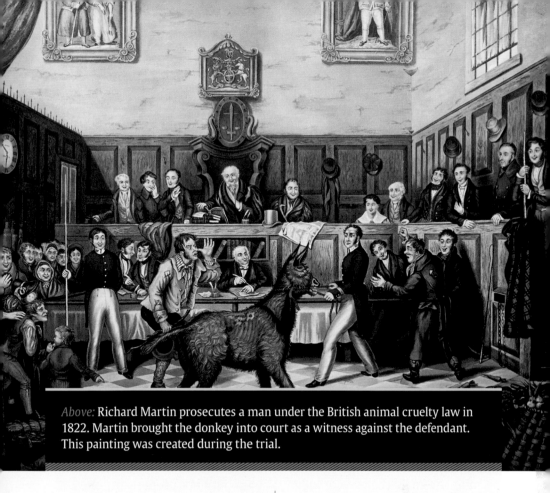

Above: Richard Martin prosecutes a man under the British animal cruelty law in 1822. Martin brought the donkey into court as a witness against the defendant. This painting was created during the trial.

The ASPCA began a crusade to provide animals with kinder, more humane treatment. One of the outcomes of this crusade was the 28-Hour Law. The U.S. Congress passed this law in 1873. It stated that animals transported to slaughterhouses by train had to be rested and given food and water every twenty-eight hours. Before the law was passed, animals were sometimes jammed into railroad cars, where they suffered for days before they were butchered.

EVOLVING LAWS

In the early 1900s, many U.S. journalists took up the fight for better laws to regulate the slaughter of animals. One of the most famous books of the time was *The Jungle*, written by Upton Sinclair in 1906. In his book, Sinclair described the

Above: Upton Sinclair (1878–1968) was an activist and author who wrote more than ninety books.

filthy and unsafe conditions of slaughterhouses in Chicago, Illinois. Animals there were killed slowly and brutally, workers clubbed them, slit their throats, and even dipped them into boiling water. The blood of both diseased and healthy animals ran everywhere, infecting and spoiling meat headed for the marketplace.

As a result of the public outcry in response to the book, Congress passed the Pure Food and Drug Act in 1906. The act regulated health standards in slaughterhouses. And yet it also resulted in more hardship for the animals. The law stated that after animals had been slaughtered, they could not be allowed to lie on slaughterhouse floors in the blood of other animals. As a consequence, animals were instead suspended by one leg from a rope or chain and then axed to death. This practice ended in 1958 when Congress passed the Humane Slaughter Act. This law required that animals be stunned before being put to death.

Despite this law, cruelty continued to take place in the slaughterhouses. Some animals were still not properly stunned, and others were abused or treated with cruelty by the workers of the slaughterhouses before stunning. Sometimes improperly functioning equipment resulted in the abuse of slaughterhouse animals. As a result of these conditions, the Humane Slaughter Act was updated in 1978 to allow U.S. government inspectors to halt slaughterhouse operations if they observed instances of animal cruelty. However, due to the expense and inconvenience of stopping slaughterhouse operations, these inspections eventually lessened and all but tapered off.

In 2001 a newspaper article in the *Washington Post* publicly charged the U.S. government with not properly enforcing the Humane Slaughter Act. The article stated that the government "has stopped tracking the number of violations and dropped all mentions of humane slaughter from its list of rotating tasks for inspectors." As a result of this article, public attention to the issue grew. In 2002 President George W. Bush signed the Farm Bill. This bill included a resolution that required the Humane Slaughter Act to be enforced. This meant that the U.S. government was required to perform regular inspections and to take action against slaughterhouses that were not humanely handling all animals.

But many people question whether these current slaughter laws adequately protect animals from unnecessary suffering. Other people wonder what difference it makes, since the animals are about to die anyway. The strictest animal rights activists say they would prefer outlawing the slaughter

Laws passed in the first half of the twentieth century regulated the way slaughterhouses *(above)* handled animals.

of animals altogether. Many Americans oppose such an idea, since it would eliminate the supply of meat and put many people involved in livestock production, such as farmers and ranchers, out of business.

Many animal welfare groups don't want to outlaw livestock production, but they tend to agree that the current laws on slaughtering the animals are not adequate and still not strictly enforced. Typically, animals that are to be slaughtered are penned together tightly while a worker stuns them, one by one, with an electric shock to the head. Then another worker hoists the animal onto something and slits each of the animals' throats. But sometimes the shock is not strong enough. Or its effect doesn't last until the animal is killed, and the animal may be conscious while hoisted or before its throat is slit.

In addition, the Humane Slaughter Act has its limits. The act applies only to slaughterhouses that sell meat to the federal government or its agencies. In addition, the act doesn't protect poultry or fish— the majority of the animals killed for food in the United States. Furthermore, in 2005, some groups began lobbying to include rabbits in the category of poultry so that the Humane Slaughter Act would not apply to the slaughter of rabbits.

In addition to these concerns, animal welfare groups also charge that the Humane Slaughter Act only protects animals from cruelty during the time of the slaughter and not during the animals' stay at the slaughterhouse. This can mean that the animals are treated cruelly before their death, even if they are ultimately slaughtered humanely.

Animal welfare groups also say that even with the law, thorough and regular inspections are still not taking place. They claim that slaughterhouse animals are routinely abused and improperly stunned. These groups would like all creatures to be given the most humane treatment before slaughter.

With changes in transportation patterns in the United States, the 28-Hour Act has also come under fire. Animals transported to slaughterhouses by train were protected by the law, but those transported by trucks were not. By the early 2000s, 95 percent of all animals transported to slaughter were taken by truck. Finally, in 2006, after years of protest from animal welfare groups, the U.S. Department of Agriculture (the USDA, which oversees and regulates farming activities) updated the law to apply to animals transported by trucks. This was a major victory for the animal welfare groups that had been asking for the change.

Despite the victories, progress in gaining rights for animals at slaughterhouses has been slow in coming. Strong lobbies representing farmers, ranchers, and meatpackers have prevented significant changes in the laws. (Lobbies are groups that try to promote favorable legislation—or defeat unfavorable legislation—for certain issues by influencing legislators and other public officials.) These lobbies claim that too much regulation of the industry needlessly drives up the cost of producing meat, an expense that is passed on to the consumer.

> " It's long past time for USDA to apply the nation's only federal humane farm animal transport law to modern-day forms of transportation. This is a not some abstract debate—the failure to apply this law to trucks is causing distress and death [of animals], and it's shameful. "
>
> —JONATHAN LOVVORN, ANIMAL PROTECTION LITIGATION AND RESEARCH, HUMANE SOCIETY OF THE UNITED STATES, 2006

www.usatoday.com

USA TODAY

Money
SECTION B

March 25, 2008

Cattle Abuse Wasn't Rare Occurrence

From the Pages of USA TODAY The abuse of non-ambulatory [fallen] cattle at a California slaughterhouse has renewed calls for a ban on the slaughter of such animals, and newly released government records show such mishandling in past years was more than a rare occurrence.

More than 10% of the humane-slaughter violations issued by the U.S. Department of Agriculture (USDA) for the 18 months ended March 2004 detailed improper treatment of animals that couldn't walk—mostly cattle, says the Animal Welfare Institute, an animal-protection group.

The finding is included in a report to be released today on humane-slaughter violations. It comes as the USDA steps up checks on conditions at the nation's 900 slaughterhouses following abuses at Westland/Hallmark Meat, now at the heart of the biggest beef recall ever.

An undercover animal-rights worker at the plant used a video camera to document workers moving downed cows with forklifts, sticking them repeatedly with electric prods and spraying water down their noses to make them stand, allegedly to get them to slaughter.

The USDA called the actions "egregious [outrageous] violations of humane-handling regulations." American Meat Institute (AMI) spokeswoman Janet Riley called them an "anomaly [unusual event]."

But the USDA records obtained by the Animal Welfare Institute (AMI) describe 501 humane-handling or slaughter violations that occurred at other slaughter plants.

THE ANIMAL WELFARE ACT

Another major federal law affecting the treatment of animals is the Animal Welfare Act. Congress passed it after animal welfare groups such as the ASPCA and the Humane Society of the United States exposed the conditions under which many laboratory animals live.

The act, which has been amended (changed) several

At one plant, a downed cow was pushed 15 feet [4.5 meters] with a forklift. Other companies were cited for dragging downed but conscious animals, letting downed cattle be trampled and stood on by others and, in one case, using "excessive force" with a rope and an electric prod to get a downed cow to stand, the enforcement records say.

What occurred at Westland/Hallmark led Sen. Dianne Feinstein, D-Calif., to introduce a bill this month to ban the slaughter of all non-ambulatory animals and shut down slaughter facilities that repeatedly violate the rules. Sen. Daniel Akaka, D-Hawaii, a co-sponsor of the bill, has sought a ban since 1992. "Animals that are sick or too weak to stand or walk on their own should not be slaughtered and used for food," Feinstein said Monday in a statement.

The AMI, the meat industry's leading trade group, opposes a ban.

Millions of pounds of wholesome meat would be lost if animals with any injury couldn't be slaughtered, it says.

The AMI estimates the number of non-ambulatory cattle affected by a ban may be as few as 25,000 a year, mostly dairy cows at the end of their milk-producing lives.

Animal-rights activists counter that a ban would increase food safety and shorten the suffering of disabled animals.

"If crippled animals cannot be sold for food, slaughter plants have no reason to prolong their misery to try to get them through the slaughter process," Wayne Pacelle, CEO of the Humane Society of the United States, recently told a congressional committee.

Like the AMI, the USDA has said that what occurred at Westland/Hallmark was an isolated case. Still, it has directed inspectors to spend more time the next six weeks checking humane-handling practices.

—Julie Schmit

times since its initial passage in 1966, sets standards for the treatment of animals used in research, zoos, circuses, and pet stores. It covers such issues as housing, food, cleanliness, and medical care. The act also states that animals used in medical research must be given drugs to prevent pain and suffering, unless the experiment depends on measurement of the animal's pain. (Some researchers study the effects of a painkiller to see how well it works, for example.)

The Animal Welfare Act requires that researchers keep accurate records on how animals are used in research. They must report how many animals were used in experiments, how many were given drugs, and how many experienced no pain or distress at all.

In addition to following these laws, most research institutes must also follow the *Guide for the Care and Use of Laboratory Animals*. It contains standards set by the National Institutes of Health (NIH). Any institution receiving U.S. Public Health Service funding must follow these standards. This regulation covers an estimated 40 percent of biomedical research in the United States. Under these regulations, committees monitor the use of animals in research.

Pro-animal groups are unhappy with the measure. They argue that mice, rats, birds, and cold-blooded animals aren't covered by the regulations of the Animal Welfare Act. These animals make up 95 percent or more of all laboratory animals, severely limiting the impact of the law. Despite pushes to protect these animals, lawmakers

Below: Animals such as these rats, as well as mice and birds, are not covered by the Animal Welfare Act. Since rats and mice make up a large percentage of lab animals, the law has limited impact.

have resisted, and these animals remain exempt from (not covered by) legal protection.

Animal rights activists also question the enforcement of the Animal Welfare Act for those animals it does cover. In 1988 the Society for Animal Protective Legislation alleged that 25 percent of all licensed animal dealers were never inspected by the USDA, the agency responsible for enforcing the regulations. To correct this situation, legislation was introduced in Congress in 1990 to provide another $12 million for enforcement. However, 1990 was a budget-tightening year. Since Congress did not think the country could afford the extra $12 million, the bill was defeated.

In 1991 Congress wrote new regulations, ordering the USDA to better enforce the terms of the Animal Welfare Act. At that time, inspectors for the USDA admitted to not knowing how to enforce the terms of the act and that much research

USA TODAY Snapshots®

Animal rights breed new area of law

Among the USA's American Bar Association-approved law schools, the number that offer courses in animal law:

Source: Charting the Growth of Animal Law in Education by Peter Sankoff; Animal Legal Defense Fund

By Anne R. Carey and Alejandro Gonzalez, USA TODAY, 2008

was needed before they could properly regulate the conditions for laboratory animals. According to the Animal Legal Defense Fund (ALDF, an organization that fights for animal rights through the legal system), almost three years later, the USDA still hadn't made good on its promise to improve conditions for the almost one hundred thousand nonhuman primates in captivity for research. So the ALDF sued the USDA in 2003. The courts dismissed the case the following year, and the ALDF's appeals since then have failed as well. The group continues the fight.

Law Injected into Animal Testing

From the Pages of
USA TODAY
Buried in the mammoth federal spending bill covering agriculture lies a mouse-size amendment that is causing a lot of roaring among biomedical scientists and animal welfare activists.

The bill, signed Saturday by President Clinton, contains language that requires the U.S. Department of Agriculture (USDA) to hold off a year before adding laboratory mice, birds and rats to the list of animals that are protected under the 1966 Animal Welfare Act.

They had long been excluded from the act, which regulates the living conditions of dogs, cats, rabbits, monkeys and other animals in laboratories. But in September, an animal rights group won a big victory when the USDA settled a long-running lawsuit by agreeing to include them. [This decision was later reversed, however, and the battle to include all animals continues.]

Animal rights groups want the provisions because, they argue, unregulated research animals all too often live under cruel conditions not allowed by the law. They say a lack of oversight leads researchers to use animals more than necessary in medical research instead of looking for alternatives.

The research community, meanwhile, argues that extending the law to cover rats, mice, and birds—which make up about 95% of laboratory animals—will require researchers to spend a fortune keeping track of redundant [repetitive] regulations, will generate thousands of pages of additional documentation and will open the door to further restrictions aimed at stopping fruitful medical research done with animals.

Researchers argue that extending the rules would end research efforts at community colleges, high schools and other institutions too poor to deal with federal regulations and inspections. Animal rights activists say institutions that can't comply shouldn't be doing research in the first place.

"We went through the system and followed the rules," says John McArdle of the Alternatives Research & Development Foundation (ARDF), one of the groups that sued the government to get the animals included under the law. "And they went through a sneaky, backdoor way to put off a judicial decision."

But the USDA's Susan McAvoy says the agency settled the lawsuit, agreeing to start a lengthy session of public meetings aimed at agreeing on new rules, just so that researchers' views could be heard. Losing the case would have meant immediate protection under the Animal Welfare Act for the more than 20 million mice, rats and birds that scientists use in biomedical research nationwide, without any discussion.

Under the act, inspectors visit labs once a year, looking at cage sizes, food and water dishes, and sanitation; checking the floor for holes and the walls for peeling paint; and randomly checking the health of animals.

Right now, 43 lab inspectors, all veterinarians, check labs holding animals that are covered by the act, including monkeys, hamsters and dogs, part of a $10.1 million annual effort. Their inspections cover about 5% of lab animals, by some estimates.

McArdle points out that one benefit of an expanded act would be an accurate census of lab mice, rats and birds. And he suggests that researchers at the largest institutions have little to fear because most already meet U.S. Public Health Service standards that match the Animal Welfare Act standards.

"Then why do it at all?" asks researcher Richard Traystman, head of the animal welfare committee at Johns Hopkins University in Baltimore. "All this does is place an unbelievable burden of paperwork on researchers, raising the cost of finding new medicines."

Under the settlement, Traystman foresees yearly changes in regulated cage sizes, mandated "environmental enrichment" toys for lab rats and researchers filling out individual forms for each of the 42,000 mice used at Johns Hopkins.

—Dan Vergano

Taking a Stand

In 2002 a Las Vegas, Nevada, sixth grader named Laurie Wolfe proved that one person can make a difference for animal rights. Her science class was dissecting (cutting open) frogs to teach the students about biology. But Wolfe refused to participate. She did not believe that killing an animal was worth the knowledge she might gain.

When her science teacher lowered her grade, Wolfe went to the county school board. There, she convinced the board of her position. The school board voted to give students the right to opt out of dissections without being penalized. It's a policy that at least eight states have adopted, as well as many local school boards.

"You don't learn anything about an animal by cutting it up," Laurie told a reporter. "It's a waste when there are so many other ways to learn about science without having to kill something first."

BEYOND THE LAW

Frustrated by the slow pace of change in the legal system, some animal rights groups have performed illegal acts in an effort to free animals in laboratories and on fur farms (places where animals are raised and killed for their fur). The Animal Liberation Front (ALF) is the most notable of these groups. Founded in the United Kingdom in 1976, ALF has an active membership in the United States. The organization has taken credit for more than one thousand criminal acts on biomedical facilities, research labs, and fur farms since its founding in the United States in 1982.

At Texas Tech University, for example, ALF members destroyed a researcher's laboratory, stole five cats, and sent the researcher a condom that they reported had been contaminated with the AIDS virus. The researcher had been using cats to study sudden infant death syndrome (SIDS), the leading killer of children under the age of one.

In addition to breaking into laboratories and freeing animals, ALF has also admitted to firebombing and vandalizing targets related to animal research in the name of animal rights. Actions such as these have earned ALF a place on the Federal Bureau of Investigation's (FBI's) list of domestic terrorists.

And although the terrorist acts of September 11, 2001, in New York and near Washington, D.C., have directed the country's attention toward foreign terrorists, the Anti-Defamation League (ADL) claims that extreme animal rights groups are one of the most active domestic terrorist movements in the United States.

ALF members and their supporters argue that violent acts are the only way to bring about meaningful change in

Above: Members of the Animal Liberation Front hold hens that they had taken from a farm.

U.S. society. The slow pace of the legal system frustrates these activists, and they feel that threats and violence produce quicker results.

A handful of extreme activists even support taking human lives to further their cause. For example, Dr. Jerry Vlasak, a surgeon and former animal researcher from California, is associated with ALF. Vlasak points to a 2006 ALF victory as evidence that force (or the threat of force) works when it comes to securing rights for animals. Vlasak was referring to a case in which ALF activists harassed a professor at the University of California at Los Angeles for years—and directly threatened the lives of his family—for research he was doing with primates. The professor eventually gave up his research. Vlasak believes that would not have happened had it not been for the direct threats from the ALF.

"I think for five lives, 10 lives, 15 human lives, we could save a million, 2 million, 10 million nonhuman lives," Vlasak said about the use of violence as a form of protest. For Vlasak and other animal rights extremists, the loss of a few human lives in the fight for animal rights is the same as the loss of human lives in the fight for the abolition of slavery in the 1800s. In the end, they say, a better world is created, and the loss of some human life is a price they are willing to pay.

Researchers, as well as most other law-abiding citizens, believe that ALF members are unethical vandals. They wonder how people who claim to care about the rights of animals can be so destructive and abuse the rights of others. How can ALF activists seemingly place more importance on the lives of animals than on the lives of people?

Most other animal welfare groups agree that violent actions such as these hurt their cause. These more moderate group members worry that acts of force carried out in the name of animal rights will give opponents of animal welfare further grounds to dismiss their concerns.

However, some nonviolent animal rights organizations such as PETA have supplied ALF with money in support of its cause. And PETA cofounder Ingrid Newkirk has applauded the actions of ALF in two of her books.

NEW LEGAL FRONTIERS

Activists continue to push for more rights for animals, with gradual success. For example, in 2001, animal rights groups persuaded the U.S. Congress to force the Environmental Protection Agency (EPA) to spend $4 million for "research, development and validation of non-animal, alternative chemical screening and prioritization methods."

> **I don't think the [animal rights protesters] who take illegal direct action . . . are looking for popular support. They do it because they know in their hearts that it's right.**
>
> **—ALF ACTIVIST DAVID BARBARASH,** WHO SERVED FOUR MONTHS IN JAIL FOR RELEASING ANIMALS FROM A LAB
>
> ● USA TODAY · NOVEMBER 12, 1998

Matthew's Rights

In 2008 Austrian courts heard a landmark case concerning animal rights. A twenty-eight-year-old chimp named Matthew Hiasl Pan was at the center of the controversy. The shelter where Matthew had lived for twenty-five years was having money troubles and was in danger of being closed. That could mean Matthew would be destroyed.

An Austrian-based group known as the Association Against Animal Factories (AAAF) went to court seeking a ruling that would declare Matthew a person and give him a similar legal status to that of a child. They wanted to have a legal guardian appointed for Matthew.

Above: Matthew Hiasl Pan was at the center of a legal battle over animal rights in Austria in 2008.

The court determined, however, that Matthew was not a person and did not have such rights. Matthew's supporters planned to appeal the decision. They also set up a foundation to pay for his care. In captivity a chimpanzee's life expectancy is about sixty years.

"I think there's a very big misunderstanding about this," said Paula Stibbe, a British animal rights advocate who had volunteered to be Matthew's legal guardian. "People imagine that we're trying to get rights for a non-human animal so he can go to college. This is about basic rights not to be killed."

Donations from around the world have paid for Matthew's continued care as the AAAF appeals the case. Because of the media attention paid to his case, it is unlikely he will be destroyed even if the AAAF loses its appeal.

Congress was telling the EPA to put more resources into developing nonanimal means of testing. It was, ultimately, a small victory, but it showed some movement in the direction of a desire for alternative methods of medical testing.

was introduced (though never voted on) in the U.S. Congress in 2008. In Europe, great apes are gaining more and more legal rights. In June 2008, for example, Spain granted these animals rights such as the right to life, freedom from arbitrary

> " **The result [of great ape protection in Europe] is that basic science on primates is effectively not possible. This research is not a luxury. . . . [The knowledge gained] cannot be accessed by experiments with humans.** "
>
> **—SWISS RESEARCHER KEVAN MARTIN,**
> 2009

The treatment of the great apes—including gorillas, bonobos, orangutans, and chimpanzees—has also been of special concern in the twenty-first century. The great apes are humanity's closest animal relatives and, according to many, should therefore get special protection. The Great Ape Protection Act

captivity, and protection from torture. In Austria a court considered a case that would grant a chimpanzee all the rights of a human being. In the end, the court rejected the idea that the chimp had rights, but that the case had been heard at all marked progress for the animal rights movement.

CHAPTER THREE

Animals and Medical Research

THE NOBEL PRIZE IS ONE OF THE HIGHEST HONORS a scientist can be awarded. So in 2007, when three scientists—Martin Evans of Wales and Americans Mario Capecchi and Oliver Smithies—were presented with the prize for their work in creating "designer mice," the world took notice. These genetically engineered lab animals could be purposely created to have a variety of genetic disorders, such as high cholesterol, diabetes, and a variety of other problems, making them ideal for medical research.

Opinions on the achievement varied widely. To many supporters of animal rights, the idea of creating animals with built-in disorders seemed outrageous. To others, it was a medical miracle. It meant that researchers would have populations of animal subjects tailor-made to suit specific areas of research.

Thomas Cech, the president of the Maryland-based Howard Hughes Medical Institute, said that

Left: A medical researcher used mice, such as this one, to create a treatment for a boy with a rare genetic disease.

while the idea of tinkering with an animal's genetics to give it targeted flaws was controversial, the rewards to humans could be rich. "There are certainly ethical concerns, which are not trivial," Cech said. "But it's a big leap from mouse to man. And when it comes to curing something like cystic fibrosis, muscular dystrophy, a devastating blood disorder, mutations that lead to cancer or Alzheimer's, there's widespread enthusiasm that if this could be done safely, some people would gain comfort."

From designer mice to cloning to transgenic animals (those with genes from other species added into their genetic code), the role of animals in medical research is hotly debated. Is it okay to sacrifice the lives and the suffering of animals to further our medical knowledge? If so, what limits should protect the animals from unnecessary suffering during such research? And how far should humans go in genetically altering the animals upon which they experiment?

THE CASE FOR USING ANIMALS IN MEDICAL RESEARCH

In 1796 British doctor Edward Jenner introduced the first effective vaccine against smallpox. This disease causes victims to suffer high fever and sores all over their bodies. It had claimed millions of lives and left countless other people blinded or badly scarred.

Above: A boy shows the symptoms of smallpox. Smallpox ravaged much of the world in the eighteenth century, until British doctor Edward Jenner introduced a vaccine in 1796.

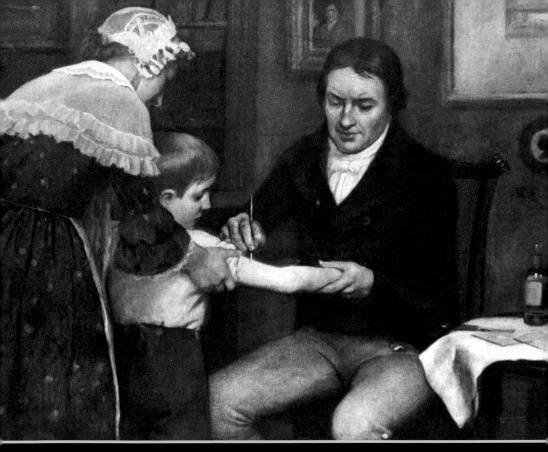

Above: In this illustration, Dr. Edward Jenner vaccinates a boy against smallpox by injecting him with cowpox.

Jenner noticed that dairy workers who became infected with cowpox, a less severe version of the disease, became immune to smallpox. Cowpox caused a few sores on the person's hands but carried little danger of disfigurement or death. In a risky experiment, Jenner took some matter from sores on the hand of Sarah Nelmes, a dairy worker who had become infected with cowpox while milking cows. Jenner then made two cuts on the arm of James Phipps, a healthy eight-year-old boy, and inserted the matter from one of Nelmes's cowpox sores. The boy became ill with cowpox. Several weeks later, Jenner inserted smallpox matter into Phipps the same way.

Phipps never got smallpox. The cowpox injection turned out to be the world's first vaccination—a medical process in which a person receives a tiny exposure to a disease, creating a natural immunity. Since the discovery of the smallpox vaccine, researchers have used animals (instead of eight-year-old boys) to develop vaccines for other human diseases such as polio, tetanus, whooping cough, measles, chicken pox, and even the flu. Without these vaccines, countless people would have died from these diseases.

Much medical knowledge has come from research on animals. The vivisections of the seventeenth century, for example, provided an understanding of some basic principles of biology. Vivisection and dissection of animals continue to shed light on biological functions, such as how the stomach absorbs food or how the brain sends messages to other parts of the body. Much of the information in biology textbooks is due largely to the use of animals in biological research. The idea of cutting open a living being to see what is going on inside remains highly controversial, however.

MEDICAL ADVANCES THROUGH RESEARCH

Researchers use animals to help them learn about the nature of diseases and other medical and psychological abnormalities and to help find cures for them. Such research saves human lives. In the 1950s, the first kidney transplants were done on dogs. In part because of this research, kidney transplants have become relatively safe for humans. In the twenty-first century, these transplants have a success rate of 95 percent. More than seventy thousand people in the United States alone are currently on a waiting list for a new kidney. Each year, about sixteen thousand Americans receive one. For those people, the procedures that resulted from animal testing are literally the difference between life and death.

The increased survival rate among cancer patients can also be attributed to animal research.

Baby Fae

On October 26, 1984, the world was shocked by the news that doctors in California had transplanted the heart of a baboon into an infant, called Baby Fae to protect her identity. Baby Fae lived for three weeks following the transplant, but ultimately, the heart did not save her life.

The revelation, followed by Baby Fae's death, created quite a stir. It gave rise to a whole new set of ethical questions concerning the use of animals, as well as questions about the differences between animals and people. Is the transplant of animal body parts into humans a medical miracle or an unholy union of human and nonhuman body parts? And what rights should the animal have? Is the life of a baboon worth sacrificing if it gives a human a small chance of living longer?

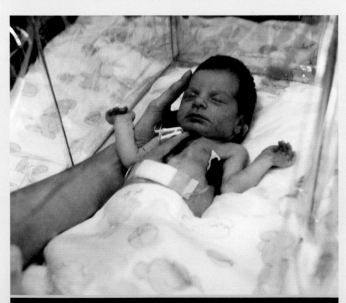

Above: Baby Fae received a baboon heart because the left side of her heart was severely underdeveloped.

In the 1930s, fewer than 20 percent of cancer patients lived more than five years after diagnosis. Improved diagnosis and treatment have helped that number climb to over half of all patients. A big part of this increase comes from anticancer drugs that were thoroughly tested on animals before being used on people. Radiation therapy for cancer has been refined through tests on rats and mice. And many surgical procedures, such as the removal of tumors, were first tested on dogs and monkeys.

Another area of research benefiting from animal testing is HIV/AIDS. This deadly disease emerged in the 1980s. At first, diagnosis was basically a death sentence. But heavy research—much of it on animals, especially nonhuman primates—have provided drugs and treatments that can greatly extend the lives of AIDS patients. Chimpanzees have been especially useful to researchers hunting for a vaccine, since they can contract the disease. Opponents of animal research point out that

400 mm³ Lewis Lung carcinoma

Endostatin therapy, Day 12

Above: These photos show a mouse with a tumor *(left)* and the same mouse twelve days later after taking experimental cancer treatments.

> " AIDS is an easy disease to avoid, but [the U.S.] government squanders millions on . . . animal tests, rather than issue frank warnings [about changes in sexual behavior], especially to young people. "
>
> —PETA VICE PRESIDENT DAN MATHEWS, 2005

vaccination studies of chimps have produced questionable results, however, because the immune systems of humans and chimps work so differently.

Treatment for kidney disease, cancer, and AIDS are just a few examples of the benefits of animal research. Researchers credit animals with playing an important role in research on nutrition, open-heart surgery, modern anesthesia, prevention and treatment of high blood pressure, ulcers, leprosy, and many other areas of medical science. Animal studies also play a big role in studying problems such as psychological imbalances, depression, sleep disorders, and much more.

Animals are also used by pharmaceutical companies to produce drugs and health supplements. For example, vitamin E can be extracted from beef liver. Horses are used to produce a serum for cholera, an intestinal disease that causes severe vomiting, diarrhea, and in extreme cases can lead to death.

A great deal of medical research also benefits animals. Many medicines and treatments developed for humans are also used to treat pets and farm animals. Pacemakers, devices that keep the heart beating, are being used in dogs and cats as well as in humans. Many animals receive chemotherapy to treat cancer, just as humans do.

Most people in the medical community believe strongly in the value of animal research and want it to continue. Surveys of doctors and scientists who belong to the American Medical Association (AMA) have revealed that the vast majority support the use of animals in basic and clinical research, as well as in drug testing. Putting a stop to using animals in medical testing, they say, would put a great damper on medical advancement.

Members of Incurably Ill for Animal Research (iiFAR) also support the current use of animals in medical research. Members of iiFAR include people who stand to benefit the most from animal experimentation— those with diseases that have so far been incurable. They believe that banning the use of animals in research would only further delay the discovery of cures for AIDS, cystic fibrosis, multiple sclerosis, Alzheimer's disease, and other serious health problems. For these people, animal research is an avenue of hope that could someday lead to a longer, disease-free life.

However, even supporters of animal research question some of the current medical research taking place. Is all of it needed? Are the results really worthwhile? In research on major diseases such as HIV and cancer, human results have time and again differed greatly from results gained in animal testing. And even when such research does provide useful results, is the loss of animal lives warranted? Some people are willing to accept that testing on rats is needed to find better medicines and techniques for treating cancer, for example, but they wonder if it is necessary to test on rats to find cures for minor health issues such as acne. Some animal rights supporters argue that in cases like these, the cost (animal life) far outweighs the gain (clearer skin).

RESEARCH VS. CRUELTY

A major milestone in animal rights awareness came in 1985, when members of ALF made public videotapes that had been stolen from a research lab at the University of Pennsylvania. The sixty hours of videotapes showed baboons with their heads cemented into plastic helmets, being knocked unconscious by a blow to the head. The tapes also showed baboons coming out of anesthesia while surgeons were still operating on their brains.

The investigation that followed revealed that the researchers had been given money from the federal government to conduct these experiments. They were supposed to have given the baboons painkillers before any injuries were inflicted. Funding for the program was stopped. The story got a great deal of publicity, and its graphic nature helped to make the question of animal welfare a more widespread concern.

Animal rights literature is filled with stories of alleged animal abuse in medical research. One article reports that monkeys at the Armed Forces Radiobiology Research Institute in Bethesda, Maryland, were used in an experiment to test the effects of radiation. The monkeys were exposed to various doses of radiation and then forced to run on a treadmill. Monkeys that stopped running on the treadmills were given electric shocks to keep them moving. Some monkeys that vomited violently during this experiment were given increasingly painful shocks to keep them moving. Some of the monkeys suffered under these conditions

Above: During a raid in California, members of ALF removed Britches, a young macaque, from a lab. PETA used images from the raid to make a video protesting animal cruelty and experimentation. This photo shows Britches after he had been nursed back to health by the ALF.

for more than five days before they finally died.

Another PETA publication shows dozens of photographs of animals used in research. One kitten is shown with an electrode implanted in its head and a gaping wound surrounding the implant. Other photos show dogs. One is pictured with its skin burned off in an experiment. Another dog, used in research on the relationship between smoking and lung cancer, is being forced to breathe nicotine-laden smoke through a tube in its throat. Tests such as these may be the minority. But they serve as a rallying point for pro-animal groups everywhere.

QUESTIONABLE METHODS?

One research method that has come under fire from animal welfare groups is the Lethal Dose 50 (LD 50) test. This method is used primarily to test potentially dangerous chemicals and new drugs. Designed in the 1920s, the classical LD 50 test calls for researchers to administer the substance in question to one hundred lab animals. The dosage is increased until fifty of the animals die—hence the name "Lethal Dose 50."

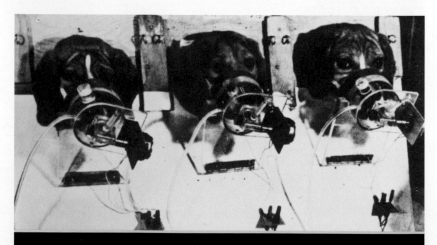

Above: This 1970s study forced dogs to breathe cigarette smoke to find out the effects of secondhand smoke.

Protesters say that this method is cruel—leading to slow and painful deaths—as well as wasteful and have campaigned to have it banned. While the test is used throughout most of the world, activists have made some progress in seeing it reduced. Some countries in Europe have banned the LD 50 outright, while in the United States, the EPA has stated that it no longer supports the test.

Many researchers say that most claims of cruelty are sensational, misleading, or both. In response to objections to the LD 50, researchers claim that few labs still use the classical LD 50 test. If a test for the lethality of a substance is necessary, researchers use as few as six subjects per test and often don't use a completely lethal dose of the substance. The animals are euthanized (killed in a painless way) as soon as they show signs of serious illness. Supporters of animal testing also point out that the Food and Drug Administration (FDA, the U.S. government agency responsible for regulating the safety of food, drugs, and other medical

The Federal Food, Drug, and Cosmetic Act

In 1937 a drug called Elixir Sulfanilamide went on the U.S. market. Two months later, more than one hundred people in fifteen states had died from taking the drug. It contained a chemical traditionally used as an antifreeze. As a result, Congress passed the Federal Food, Drug, and Cosmetic Act of 1938. It requires that any new drug be proved safe before it can be sold in the United States. Since then animal testing has become the primary way of meeting the requirements of this law.

products) requires that a food, drug, or other chemical be proved safe before it can be used on humans. Without testing on animals first, supporters say, there is a great risk that human lives would be in danger.

Pro-animal groups argue that the use of the LD 50 is still widespread. Furthermore, they contend that results from the test are unreliable, and alternatives do exist. The Fixed Dose Procedure (FDP) produces results using fewer animals with less cruelty, proponents claim. In an FDP, researchers use ten to twenty animals, and instead of measuring mortality, researchers look only for evidence of toxicity. The cost of animal suffering and lives for the FDP is significantly less than for the LD 50, and many argue that the results are just as good.

Researchers who favor animal testing insist that most animals are comfortable during research procedures. A USDA study reported that 95 percent of animals in federally funded facilities do not experience pain or distress. Of the remaining animals, most were involved in pain studies. According to the report, pain relievers or anesthesia were administered to these animals as soon as it was appropriate to do so.

Most animal researchers also follow guidelines set by the federal government to give animals good care while in captivity. Each institution has an Animal Care and Use Committee. This committee usually includes at least one veterinarian and one person who is not a part of the institution. The committee verifies that animal research is necessary and appropriate when used. It also makes sure the species being tested is appropriate and sees that no animals experience unnecessary pain or discomfort.

Animal rights activists dispute the validity of such claims. They argue that the USDA does not regulate the use of the vast majority of laboratory animals, including rats, mice, fish, and farm animals. These animals make up 95 percent or more of all lab animals. Activists wonder what good the Animal

> " I can attest that animal research is inherently cruel. Animal protection laws do not mitigate [lessen] this reality. Whether the debate involves humane issues or human benefits, the evidence confirms the need to replace animal experiments with more accurate methods. That's the best way to make progress and improve health. "

—JOHN J. PIPPIN, SENIOR MEDICAL AND RESEARCH ADVISER WITH THE PHYSICIANS COMMITTEE FOR RESPONSIBLE MEDICINE

USA TODAY · DECEMBER 15, 2008

Welfare Act is when it deliberately leaves out the majority of animals that need protection. Animal rights activists also claim that there are not enough inspectors to verify that labs are following regulations.

What is the solution? Some animal welfare advocates would like to see animals used sparingly and only in painless experiments when absolutely necessary. However, many animal rights activists believe that animals are no longer needed in medical research. They believe that researchers have many alternatives available to them and that these alternatives should be used.

CLONING

Cloning is one of the most controversial subjects in medical research. A clone, generally speaking, is an artificially produced, identical genetic copy of another animal (although scientists can also clone individual cells, rather than entire organisms). For decades, cloning was the stuff of science fiction, but that changed in 1997 when Scottish researchers introduced the first cloned mammal—a sheep named Dolly—to the world.

Life

SECTION D

February 24, 1997

HELLO DOLLY! Breakthrough with Sheep Could Herald Human Cloning

From the Pages of USA TODAY

Scientists for the first time have cloned an adult mammal using DNA from a 6-year-old sheep to create a genetically identical lamb.

The achievement, thought impossible by most experts, used the type of cloning that has been grist for science-fiction mills for decades. It also sets the stage for possibly cloning human beings, although many technical and ethical hurdles remain before that can become a reality.

"It is a landmark discovery in terms of animal development," says Colin Stewart of the National Cancer Institute-Frederick Cancer Research and Development Center in Frederick, Maryland.

"Plant biologists have always known that it's possible to clone plants from single cells. But this shows now you can do it in animals, including higher mammals like sheep."

The successful experiment by Ian Wilmut and colleagues of the Roslin Institute, Edinburgh, Scotland, will be reported in the Thursday issue of the British science journal *Nature*. Experts say it has many significant implications.

Stewart, who wrote an editorial on the research for *Nature*, told *USA TODAY* that it will be possible to create clones of animals for biomedical research as well as clones of commercial farm animals, such as dairy cows that give the greatest yield of milk.

Many people are horrified at the idea of cloning an animal, to say nothing of the prospect of creating human clones. But the idea opened up new possibilities to medical research. Researchers could run tests on large populations of genetically identical subjects. This greatly reduces the number of variables that researchers have to weigh against their results.

Since Dolly was born in 1997, scientists have cloned many

It also will provide insight into how DNA performs during fertilization, embryonic development and old age. And it will enhance the understanding of how human diseases develop and how to make better drugs to treat them.

"It has implications for the way one will think about the molecular basis of aging, and certainly it will further our understanding of how embryos develop," Stewart says. "Scientifically, it's been an extraordinary development."

Before the technique is used commercially—or before humans are cloned—it will have to be fine-tuned.

Above: Dolly at seven months old. The birth of Dolly made headlines around the world in 1997.

"The technique is still extremely inefficient," says Stewart. "They had to start with 300 eggs to get one lamb born." Nor is it clear "that this is feasible in humans."

—Tim Friend

species, including cats, mice, monkeys, cattle, horses, and more. The knowledge gained from creating these clones could one day lead to human cloning. Some people imagine a day when scientists can clone replacement organs for people. A heart or kidney cloned from one's own DNA would not be rejected by the body. The medical possibilities are endless but so are the moral and ethical questions behind such an action.

ALTERNATIVES TO ANIMAL RESEARCH

As sensitivity to animal welfare has grown over the past several decades, the push to find alternative methods of testing has grown. For example, microorganisms can sometimes be exposed to chemicals to determine whether a substance is poisonous or carcinogenic (cancer causing). The Ames test uses *Salmonella*. These single-celled organisms have no nervous system and can therefore feel no pain. Another alternative involves mathematical or computer models to simulate cell reactions and biological functions.

As another alternative, researchers sometimes use cell and tissue cultures extracted from humans or animals rather than expose a whole animal to testing. If these in vitro samples

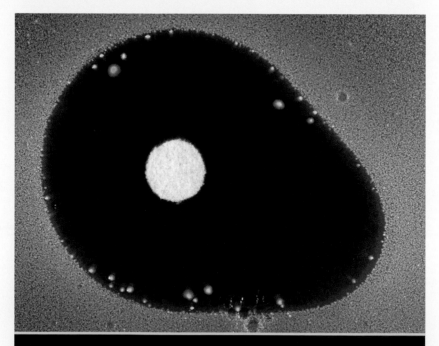

Above: This photo shows a *Salmonella* bacterial culture being used in the Ames test to see if a chemical is poisonous or carcinogenic.

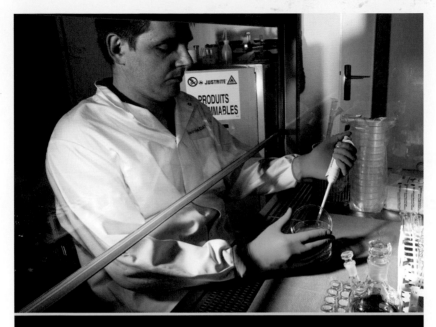

Above: A researcher adds toxins to a cell culture so that he can study the effects on the cells. Cell culture studies are a growing alternative to animal testing in toxicity and cancer studies.

are not already naturally diseased, the cells in a piece of extracted tissue can then be exposed to disease or untested drugs. The U.S. National Disease Research Interchange provides more than 120 types of human tissue to researchers who study a wide range of human diseases. This method has proved especially useful in testing for cancer and HIV/AIDS drugs. In leukemia testing, for example, researchers used to inject mice with leukemia cells so they would develop the disease. The mice were then treated with various experimental drugs. Modern researchers can test the same drugs on live human cancer cells in a test tube. The test has meant that millions of animals per year can be spared.

Pro-animal groups argue that nonanimal tests are faster, easier, and less expensive than animal testing. Furthermore, they argue that the results are more reliable. One area of nonanimal testing showing great promise is stem cells. These cells have some remarkable properties, such as the ability to grow into almost any type of cell in the body. While the use of human stem cells in testing remains politically controversial, animal stem cells can produce results. For example, stem cells from mice have proved useful in toxicity studies.

and cell cultures is often less costly for researchers than keeping animals in the laboratory. But the reliability of all these alternatives is still debatable. Researchers caution that tests done with cell and tissue cultures can be misleading. Such tests cannot be used to predict how all the parts of a human or animal biological system will react to a drug.

On the other hand, supporters of alternative testing argue, animal testing can be just as

> ❝ **The fact is, the mouse is an imperfect model of the human being. If it was perfect, it would be a person. I don't think we have much choice [but to test on animals].** ❞
>
> **—KEN PAIGEN,** HEAD OF JACKSON LABORATORY, A LEADING GENETICS LAB, 2000

Many researchers argue that alternatives to animal testing are indeed promising and attractive. But they also caution that the alternatives have their limitations. Using microorganisms

ineffective. The painkiller Vioxx was successfully tested on six different animal species before it was declared safe for human beings in 1999. The animal studies, however, failed to reveal

> **"The history of cancer research has been a history of curing cancer in the mouse. . . . We have cured mice of cancer for decades, and it simply didn't work in humans."**
>
> **—RICHARD KLAUSNER,**
> FORMER DIRECTOR OF THE NATIONAL CANCER INSTITUTE
> **USA TODAY · MARCH 30, 2007**

that the drug could drastically increase a patient's risk of heart attack or stroke. The FDA estimated that the drug contributed to somewhere between 88,000 and 139,000 heart attacks over a period of about five years. The drug was pulled from the shelves in 2004.

Another drug safely tested on animals was TGN1412. It was developed to treat leukemia, among other diseases. But in human beings, the drug caused catastrophic organ failure. The monkeys on which the drug had been tested could withstand five hundred times the dose that could be fatal to a person. The differing results between animal testing and human use in drugs like Vioxx and TGN1412 suggest that while alternative testing methods may be imperfect, so too is animal testing.

CHAPTER FOUR

Animals and Agriculture

WHEN SINGER JESSICA SIMPSON PUT ON A T-SHIRT that read "Real Girls Eat Meat," in 2008, she didn't know what she was getting into. Many people believe that the T-shirt was a joke Simpson was making at the expense of fellow singer Carrie Underwood. Underwood was a vegetarian and also the ex-girlfriend of Dallas Cowboys quarterback Tony Romo—the man in Simpson's life.

PETA members didn't think the joke was funny, and they let Simpson know how they felt. The group released an altered photograph of Simpson. In the doctored photo, the T-shirt read, "Only Stupid Girls Eat Meat," and listed "five reasons why only stupid girls eat meat."

PETA and other proponents of vegetarianism oppose eating meat not only because of the loss of animal life but also because of the way animals are treated before they are slaughtered for human consumption. They

Left: Cattle graze on a farm in Virginia. Most Americans eat meat, but a growing number of people are becoming vegetarians and vegans.

point to what they see as deplorable conditions at slaughterhouses, the lack of legal protection for animals such as chickens and turkeys, and evidence of animal abuse at large-scale farms and slaughterhouses. To make matters worse, they say, the everyday lives of many of these animals may be even worse than what they face at slaughter.

FACTORY FARMS

A big part of the objection to producing and eating meat centers on the treatment of animals in large, automated farms. Animal rights activists often call such farms "factory farms," and they believe that animals involved in such operations are treated cruelly. People in agribusiness—those who run large, automated

Above: An employee at a large factory farm collects eggs from hens. Intensive farming practices produce much of the world's food supply.

Above: Free-range chickens roam around an organic farm in Minnesota. Many people view free-range practices as the return to old-fashioned family farming.

farms—refer to their industry as "intensive farming."

At Maybury State Park in Northville, Michigan, state officials have set up what they call a living farm. A walk through the farm provides visitors with a look at life on an old-fashioned family farm. Geese and ducks swim in a large pond, cows graze in spacious pastures, and pigs lie in their pens. Dozens of hens roost together in a small shed, laying their eggs where they please. A farm employee throws the animals hay and grain that are grown at the farm. The employee frequently pets the animals or calls them by name. Visitors can see workers sheering sheep for their wool, extracting honey from a hive, and much more.

Farms like the one in Maybury State Park were once quite common. With such an operation, a farmer could generally raise enough food to feed four or five people. Some small farms still exist, but they are not responsible for the great amount of food produced in the United States. Large family-owned and company-owned farms are responsible for that.

Free-Range Meat

Decades ago, almost all cattle ranchers raised free-range meat. The cattle were allowed to graze on natural grasses. But over time, many large cattle producers stopped this practice. Finding grazing land was costly and time consuming. Cattle could be more easily penned and fed in feedlots.

Recently, however, a movement toward free-range cattle has started. Feedlot animals have a higher rate of disease, and this affects the healthfulness and quality of the meat. Free-range meat is more expensive, but many proponents point out that it's of higher quality. In addition, many animal rights advocates believe the treatment of free-range cattle is more humane. The cattle are allowed to roam, rather than stay penned in cramped quarters. Free-range movements in poultry and egg production are also gaining steam.

Animal rights groups support the movement but also caution that the label "free range" on packaging can be misleading. For example, for poultry to be legally labeled free range, the birds must have some access to the outdoors, but there's no restriction on how much (or how little). This means that the consumer can't really find out just how much freedom the animals have been granted. Stricter definitions are needed for the "free range" label to be truly meaningful, animal rights supporters argue.

As farming became less common as a way of life, it became more and more important as a business. In the twenty-first century, less than 2 percent of all Americans live on farms, yet production is greater than ever before. In 1945 producing one hundred bushels of corn required about fourteen hours of labor. By the 2000s, with mechanization of farming, the same amount required only three hours of labor. Whether for growing grain or raising livestock, large-scale farming is by far the most efficient and least expensive way to go. The development of genetics—the biological science that explains how physical characteristics are inherited—has allowed farmers to improve breeding methods. Improved livestock feeds, mechanization of feeding and slaughtering techniques, and advances in veterinary medicine have further increased productivity. Large-scale cattle facilities, often called feedlots, produce cattle at rates small farms can never hope to match. In the twenty-first century, the United States has an estimated 258 feedlots producing more than two-thirds of the nation's cattle every year.

THE BENEFITS OF INTENSIVE FARMING

To get such high productivity for the lowest cost, farmers use automation whenever possible. In a typical broiler chicken farm, for example, young chicks are penned in groups of ten thousand or more. Sometimes the chicken houses have tiers to maximize space. Food and water are dropped automatically from feeders in the roof of the pen. Small amounts of antibiotics and growth hormones are added to the food. These additives help to fight off disease and also increase the rate of growth among the birds. The

Below: Feedlots, such as this one in New Mexico, supply meat to much of the United States as well as other parts of the world.

chickens are usually ready for the market in about seven weeks.

The average American, who eats more than 60 pounds (27 kilograms) of beef and 50 pounds (23 kg) of chicken each year, benefits financially from large, efficiently run, automated farms. Because the meat is produced in volume at relatively low cost, producers are able to charge consumers lower prices. Not only do U.S. farmers provide more than enough food for the United States, but they also export billions of dollars of meat, eggs, and other animal products to other countries. Many people believe that without modern farming techniques, farms would not be profitable, American eating habits would change drastically, and people in other countries would be denied products they desire.

USA TODAY Snapshots®

Nothing to cluck at

Americans' per-capita consumption of meats and poultry in 2008:

(in pounds)

Poultry 104.3
Beef 63
Pork 48.7
Lamb 1
Veal 0.5

Source: U.S. Department of Agriculture, February 2009

By Anne R. Carey and Suzy Parker, USA TODAY, 2009

Skyrocketing Demand

The world's meat supply in 1961 was an estimated 71 million tons (64 million metric tons). By 2007 that figure had exploded to 284 million tons (258 million metric tons).

PETA vs. Fast Food

PETA and other pro-animal groups have successfully pressured many fast-food chains into improving treatment for the animals that provide meat for their restaurants. Hardee's and Carl's Jr. both agreed to buy eggs and pork from cage-free suppliers, while Burger King has vowed to buy a greater portion of its pork and eggs from such suppliers.

Perhaps most famously, PETA sued the parent company of Kentucky Fried Chicken (KFC) over reported abuses from their chicken vendors. As a result, KFC issued animal welfare guidelines to be followed by vendors that supplied chickens to the chain.

Above: PETA activists protest outside of a Kentucky Fried Chicken in Los Angeles, California, in 2008.

DOES INTENSIVE FARMING MEAN CRUELTY TO ANIMALS?

For the strictest animal rights activists, raising any animal to be killed and eaten is cruel. They believe that both humans and animals have a right to life. In their view, vegetarianism or veganism (consuming no animal by-products, including dairy) are the only ways to ensure this right.

Many animal welfare groups have no objection to animals being raised for food, but they object to the methods used to raise and slaughter them. For example, the Humane Farming Association (HFA), a nonprofit organization of public health specialists, veterinarians, consumer advocates, and family farmers, has more than 190,000 members. The HFA's goals are "to protect farm animals from cruelty, to protect the public from the dangerous misuse of antibiotics, hormones, and other chemicals used on factory farms, and to protect the environment from the impacts of industrialized animal factories."

One of the HFA's most successful campaigns has been against the methods used by many large farms to raise milk-fed calves for veal. About one million milk-fed calves are raised in the United States each year. These calves are taken away from their mothers when they are a few days old and placed in crates that are approximately 22 inches (56 centimeters) wide and 58 inches (147 cm) long. The calves are fed low-iron milk for fourteen to sixteen weeks, and then they are sent to market for slaughter. Because of their diet and lack of exercise, the calves grow to 300 pounds (136 kg) or more by slaughter time. The meat from these calves, called veal, is pale white in color, very tender, and flavorful.

Animal rights activists and the HFA say that the trade-off for the human consumption of white veal is the comfort and health of the animals. The crates they are kept in, says the HFA, are too small for the animals to turn around. Eventually, the cramped quarters and the lack of exercise cripple many calves. The low-iron milk diet results in diarrhea and anemia (a lack

Above: These veal calves are kept inactive in crates so that their muscles don't develop too much and their meat stays tender.

of vitality due to a deficiency of red blood cells). Activists also argue that drugs and chemicals fed to the calves get into the meat, making it of questionable healthfulness to the consumer. The HFA and many animal rights groups have called for consumers to boycott veal. According to the HFA's website, the boycott is working, with veal sales down almost 70 percent in recent years. The public's idea about veal has changed so much that the American Veal Association has changed the definition of what can be called veal. In the twentieth century, the reddish meat of calves allowed to go outside and eat grass could not be called veal. That changed in the mid-2000s. In fact, more and more of the veal on grocery store shelves wouldn't have even been labeled veal at the turn of the century.

Veal calves aren't the only animals to suffer in factory farms, according to animal welfare activists. In his book

Inhumane Society, veterinarian Dr. Michael Fox claims that the crowded conditions on "factory farms" lead to high stress in animals, which causes violent behavior among the animals. To reduce fighting, farmers often use a laser instrument to cut off the beaks of hens. According to Fox, piglets often have their tails amputated (called tail docking) to prevent tail biting and cannibalism among the pigs. These are just a few examples of many that animal welfare activists point to as examples of animal suffering on factory farms.

THE RESPONSE OF THE ANIMAL INDUSTRY

The Animal Agriculture Alliance is a group of individuals and companies involved in industrial farming. The Alliance works to educate people about intensive farming, claiming that large

Poultry farmers often debeak chicken and turkey hens *(above)* to keep them from pecking one another when they are in close quarters.

farms do all they can to ensure the well-being of their animals. They add that industrial farms are critical to the food supply of the nation and the world.

"The average American is now at least three generations removed from the farm and has become dependent on supermarkets and restaurants to supply almost all of his/her food needs," says the Alliance.

the defensive and must become proactive in order to make a real impact."

Some large-scale farmers claim that the treatment animals receive on large, automated farms is actually more humane than treatment received on a small, family-run operation. On small farms, animals are raised primarily outdoors, where they are exposed to bad weather and

> " A new dairy [facility] would be a happy place to be a cow. They have roofs to protect from summer heat and winter rain, comfortable stalls and clean bedding. "
>
> —**JIM REYNOLDS,** CHAIR OF THE AMERICAN ASSOCIATION OF BOVINE PRACTITIONERS' ANIMAL WELFARE COMMITTEE
>
> **USA TODAY · DECEMBER 11, 2002**

"Because of the success of animal agriculture, the public has heard little with regard to animal well-being. . . . The positive message of feeding the world safely and inexpensively doesn't sell papers or network advertising. Therefore, animal agriculture has often found itself on

extreme temperatures, predators, and disease. On most large farms, animals are sheltered and receive the best food and health care possible. The foundation points out that if animals were truly stressed, they would not become fat, lay eggs, or give milk.

Likewise, other practices that animal rights groups view as cruel are thought by farmers to be kind and done only to protect the animals. For example, according to those in the intensive farming industry, the the animals engage in natural behaviors.

Farming groups also argue that farmers amputate, or dock, pigs' tails for the animals' protection. Animal rights groups claim that pigs on large farms

> " **Pigs live by the hundreds of thousands in warehouse-like barns, in rows of wall-to-wall pens. . . . They trample each other to death. There is no sunlight, straw, fresh air, or earth. The floors are slatted to allow excrement [animal waste] to fall into a catchment pit under the pens.** "
>
> —*ROLLING STONE* REPORTER JEFF TIETZ, 2006

practice of debeaking chickens protects them from their own natural tendencies to attack one another. Chickens establish their rank in the flock, often called the "pecking order," by fighting. Once established, the strongest bird gets to eat first, the next strongest goes next, and so on. Debeaking the chickens eliminates the possibility of injury as try to bite off one another's tails because confinement frustrates them. But a study at Texas Tech University found that tail biting occurred among animals raised in dirt lots as well, though somewhat less frequently than with confined pigs. This evidence suggests that confinement is not the only cause of tail biting.

IS THE FOOD HEALTHY?

Animal rights advocates argue that the meat from large, automated farms is unhealthy. Food hormones and antibiotics are given regularly to confined animals to foster growth and ward off disease. As a consequence, high residues of these drugs are sometimes found in meat. The USDA reports that milk-fed veal is three times more likely to contain illegal levels of antibiotic residue than all other varieties of veal. In some cases, residue levels have been five hundred times over the legal limit. Sulfamethazine, a known cancer-causing chemical, has also been found in milk-fed veal. Some animal rights groups claim that a human's health may be endangered by eating such veal.

Pro-animal groups also argue that the USDA cannot adequately check all meats for drug residue. As few as one in two thousand cattle are actually checked. Those numbers are even lower for hogs and poultry.

Below: USDA inspectors visit a meatpacking plant in Nebraska in 2008.

November 3, 2008

Agribusiness Fights Prop. 2

From the Pages of
USA TODAY

SAN FRANCISCO—A California ballot measure to improve conditions for farm animals has generated national opposition from agribusiness interests.

If passed Tuesday, Proposition 2 would prevent California farmers from confining egg-laying hens, pregnant pigs and veal calves in ways that don't allow them to lie, stand and extend their limbs.

The proposal has grown into the most expensive animal-rights ballot measure ever, with both sides raising almost $8 million each. Some opponents are concerned that it could spur national changes.

"If it passes in California, Oregon will be the next one . . . and it'll spread through the nation," says Gordon Satrum, co-owner of Willamette Egg Farms in Canby, Ore.

Other measures banning restrictive crates for pigs and veal calves have passed in Florida, Arizona, Colorado and Oregon. California will be the test case for hens. The state doesn't have much of a veal or pork industry but supplies almost 6% of the nation's eggs.

Proposition 2 opponents, who include some poultry veterinarians and academic experts, say the changes would drive egg prices far higher and put California producers out of business because they couldn't compete with out-of-state rivals or Mexican imports.

Proposition 2 supporters say it's inhumane to keep hens, pigs and calves in crates slightly larger than their bodies. They also say the changes, to be phased in by 2015, may lead to only small increases in egg prices and that salmonella [harmful bacteria] risks drop when hens are not caged. The proposition doesn't require the hens to be outdoors, they say, so no increased avian flu risk is likely.

Current conditions "immobilize animals" and prevent natural behaviors, says Wayne Pacelle, CEO of the Humane Society. He says pigs and calves are confined such that they can't turn around, and that caged hens are "living on top of each other."

He says Proposition 2 would hasten the industry's shift to cage-free eggs, which more buyers want but which cost about 25% more at retail and account for less than 5% of the market.

Today's industry standards call for caged hens to get at least 67 square inches [432 sq. cm] of space each, a little less than a regular-size sheet of paper. Hens are typically caged in groups of two to eight.

The measure's opponents say that, if interpreted strictly, the proposition would require more than 5 square feet [0.5 sq. m] of space per hen so they can all stretch wings at the same time.

"We don't have enough land," to do that, says Ryan Armstrong, of the family-owned Armstrong Egg Farms near San Diego. "We'll be out of business."

His 60-year-old company has 660,000 hens; 9% are cage free. He says the measure would require Armstrong to reduce its hen count by two-thirds or invest $20 million. That may not be feasible and would lead to higher egg prices.

Pacelle says the claim that the proposition requires all hens to be able to extend their wings at the same time is "ludicrous." On its website, Proposition 2 supporters say that claim displays the "level of the desperation that factory farms will go to."

—Julie Schmit

Because most farms are so large, regulation sometimes seems impossible. Many animal rights activists believe the only answer is to scale down or eliminate the factory farm.

People who successfully operate large farms don't deny that they use drugs on animals. Instead, they claim that the drugs are necessary for the health of the animals. The drugs, they say, would be required whether the animals were raised in shelters or outside. They also scoff at the idea that these drugs are dangerous to humans. The FDA regulates the type and amount of antibiotics given to animals so they are the same as those prescribed for humans. The FDA denies claims that its inspections are inadequate.

Farmers who operate large, automated farms also insist that no proof exists that the drugs or growth hormones given to animals cause cancer or other illnesses in humans. In fact, they say that meat is healthy for humans. Red meat is the only complete source of all ten essential amino acids, a group of organic compounds that are necessary for the proper functioning of the human body. Although studies indicate that eating too much red meat can be a health risk, eliminating red meat altogether can also be a health risk if a meatless diet is not properly balanced. Regardless of the health benefits or drawbacks, meat is a staple of the American diet, and that's unlikely to change soon.

ENVIRONMENTAL IMPACT

Intensive farming can also have an impact on the environment. The resources needed to sustain huge farms puts a huge drain on

> **A vegetarian diet can be very healthy if it's done intelligently.**
>
> —ELIZABETH TURNER, EDITOR OF *VEGETARIAN TIMES* MAGAZINE
> USA TODAY · OCTOBER 15, 2007

natural resources such as water, and the waste products of such an effort can be polluting to the environment. The Worldwatch Institute, an environmental research organization, says that it takes 5 pounds (2.3 kg) of grain, 2,500 gallons (9,500 liters) of water, the energy equivalent of 1 gallon (3.8 liters) of gasoline, and 35 pounds (16 kg) of eroded topsoil to produce a 1-pound (0.5 kg) steak. Other statistics suggest that livestock consumes half the crops grown and over half the water consumed in the United States each year. By comparison, soybeans—a protein alternative—requires less than one-fifth as much water to produce the same amount of food energy.

Above: A Louisiana farmer examines his soybean crop. Soybeans are one of the best and most easily produced alternatives to meat as a source of protein.

Veganism is Taking Root

**From the Pages of
USA TODAY**
It's hip to be a vegan: Best-selling books tout the no-meat, no-eggs, no-dairy eating style. Celebrities such as actress Natalie Portman and former presidential candidate Dennis Kucinich reportedly eat the vegan way, for reasons ranging from ethics to weight control.

So veganism is in. But is it healthy?

Short answer: Yes, it can be. But there are a few catches. The biggest is that you must be willing, at least at first, to do much more food homework than average fast-food-eating Americans.

"A lot of individuals are interested in trying this," says Keri Gans, a registered dietitian in New York City and spokeswoman for the American Dietetic Association (ADA). "Unfortunately, they don't all do the necessary research that can make it a healthy choice."

Gans says some under-informed newbie vegans end up just plain hungry, attempting to subsist on salads and soy milk. Others "end up gaining weight because they eat too many carbohydrates from pasta and rice or too many fatty nuts and seeds," says Tara Gidus, a registered dietitian in Orlando, who also is an ADA spokeswoman.

"Appropriately planned" vegetarian and vegan diets have nutritional advantages, including low levels of saturated fat and cholesterol, says a 2003 position statement from the ADA (at eatright.org).

But a poorly planned vegan diet could fall short on some key nutrients, including:

- Protein. Plant foods can provide plenty—and, no, you don't have to eat your rice and beans together to get the right mix. But you should eat a variety of foods, including whole grains, beans and nuts, to replace the proteins in meat, milk and eggs, Gidus says.
- Calcium. Dark, leafy green vegetables, such as broccoli and bok choy, contain quite a bit, but not as much as milk or cheese. Even figs, almonds and soy foods have some. But most vegans will need fortified foods (such as soy milk or orange juice) and a supplement to get enough, Gidus says. Although some vegans say they need less calcium

because their overall diets are better for bones, the ADA says they need as much as anyone.

- Vitamin D. The "sunshine vitamin" is good for bones, and emerging research suggests it may also help prevent certain cancers and heart disease. The main source in the U.S. diet: milk. The sun is a good source, too, but not always in winter or for dark-skinned people. So many vegans will need fortified foods or supplements.
- Vitamin B-12. This essential vitamin is only in animal foods. So vegans need a supplement or fortified foods.

The good news is that a basic multivitamin and a bountiful variety of fruits, vegetables, whole grains, nuts, seeds and a few fortified products—increasingly available in regular grocery stores—can cover these bases. But you will need to read labels, quiz waiters and, Gans says, become "a fairly adventurous eater." Those who live outside urban areas may also need online sources (such as Veganstore.com and VeganEssentials.com) for some items, says John Cunningham, a vegan and consumer research manager at the Vegetarian Resource Group (vrg.org).

Gans says: "People who choose this diet just because they think it might help them lose weight are going to have a hard time sticking with it. It takes commitment."

But eating a healthy vegan diet "is not difficult once you get used to it," says Jack Norris, a vegan and registered dietitian who offers tips at VeganHealth.org.

Cunningham says: "There is a little learning curve, though once you get down a core repertoire of foods and meal plans, it's really not a big deal."

—Kim Painter

Why Vegetarian?

In 2006 *Time* magazine asked vegetarians to give their main reason for their lifestyle choice.

Health: 32%
Because of chemicals and hormones in meat products: 15%
Don't like the taste of meat: 13%
Love of animals: 11%
Animal rights: 10%
Religious reasons: 6%
Environmental reasons: 4%
Weight loss: 3%
Other: 6%

Many environmentalists argue that the land, water, and grain used to feed cattle would be better used to raise soybeans, rice, wheat, corn, and other grains. The crops would feed more people in what they consider a more environmentally sound way.

Animal farmers take the opposite view. They believe that if they stopped raising cattle, the result could be an ecological disaster. Farmers also point out that the high beef production in the United States is a direct result of consumer demand. They see the reduction or elimination of meat intake as an intrusion on the personal choices and rights of U.S. consumers.

WHAT LIES AHEAD?

What is the future of large, automated farms? The EPA estimates that of all the farms in the United States, about 90 percent are family owned, while only 3 percent are corporate farms (with the remaining 7 percent group owned). Yet the largest 2 percent of U.S. farms produce more than 50 percent of the nation's total agricultural products (including grain, meat, dairy, and eggs). Clearly, intensive farming is by far the most profitable means of farming.

The demand for meat both in the United States and abroad makes intensive farming a necessity, say supporters of the meat industry. But protesters don't agree. While progress has been slow, animal rights activists have won some ground in recent years. For example, in January 2009, U.S. lawmakers introduced the Prevention of Equine Cruelty Act. It would outlaw the slaughter of horses for human consumption. If the law passes, it will end the suffering of hundreds of thousands of horses in slaughterhouses. (The demand for horse meat in the United States is low, but the meat is commonly exported to other countries.)

The legal battles concerning the raising and slaughter of food animals will likely continue for decades. Striking a balance between the need to feed the nation (and the world) and treating animals with consideration and respect is difficult, especially with limited funding to enforce the laws that are already in place.

CHAPTER FIVE

Animals in the Fashion and Cosmetic Industries

ANIMALS HAVE LONG PLAYED A PART IN THE HUMAN quest to look beautiful and fashionable. For example, ancient Egyptians concocted beauty creams for the skin. The creams were made of 90 percent animal fat and 10 percent balsam, a plant resin. Ancient Babylonians ground dried insects called cochineal into a red paste to color the lips.

In western Europe during the Middle Ages (about A.D. 500–1500), animal skins became a symbol of wealth and fashion. At that time, royalty and the upper class began to wear ermine, otter, sable, and fox furs to emphasize their social position. To name just a few examples, the plumes of peacocks and ostriches, the skins of cows and eels, and the ivory tusks of elephants have also been used in the name of fashion.

With the increase in the use of plant-based fabrics such as cotton and the development of synthetic

Left: Wearing fur has been a sign of royalty and wealth since the Middle Ages. This portrait of British king George III (1738–1820) shows him in full regal robes trimmed in ermine.

A Bloody Trade

Ivory, harvested from the tusks of elephants, has long been valued by many cultures. It has been used in everything from jewelry to piano keys to billiard balls. But the cost of ivory harvesting is heavy. Most African and Asian countries with wild elephant populations have passed laws to protect the animals. But illegal hunters, or poachers, ignore the laws, killing elephants by the thousands for their tusks. Photographs and videos show brutal images of fields of dead elephants with their tusks cut off. The rest of the animal is left to rot.

The ivory trade worldwide was once lively. But as people have become educated about the cost of ivory in animal suffering, the market has all but disappeared. A worldwide ban went into effect in 1990. The popular online auction site eBay banned all ivory sales in 2007—even for secondhand ivory. Still, a black market (illegal trade) of the substance remains, and as long as there are willing buyers, wild elephants remain in danger.

fabrics, the need to use animal skins for clothing has been greatly reduced since ancient times. But animal skins remain popular. From fur coats and shawls to leather jackets, shoes, and gloves, animal-based clothing remains a very large market in the fashion industry.

THE USE OF ANIMALS IN COSMETICS

The use of animals in the fashion industry isn't limited to just their skins. Animals are also used to test the safety of cosmetic products. Everyday products, such as eye shadow, hair spray, face cream, and shampoo, are tested to ensure that they will not cause irritation or severe damage to the skin, eyes, or internal system when used by humans.

In many ways, the use of animals in the cosmetic industry is similar to the use of animals in medical research. But there's one key difference. Medical studies, for the most part, work to further the health and well-being of people. Cosmetic testing, on the other hand, exists not to save lives but to create products that promote beauty and earn a profit for their manufacturers. Many people who advocate the use of animals in medical research may feel differently about their use in cosmetic testing.

Two tests commonly used for cosmetics are the LD 50 and the Draize test. The Draize test was developed in the 1940s by Dr. J. H. Draize of the FDA to test eye irritants. The need for such a test became evident when an untested product called Lash Lure came on the U.S. market in 1933. Lash Lure was an eyelash dye. Women who accidentally got the substance in their eyes suffered permanent eye damage.

The Draize test typically requires six rabbits. The researcher puts a yoke (restraint) around the neck of each rabbit and immobilizes its legs. The researcher then clips the eyelid of each rabbit and places

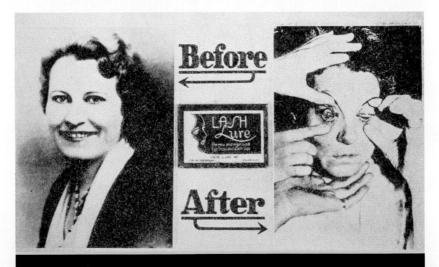

Above: This FDA poster from the 1930s warns about the dangers of Lash Lure. It shows the before and after photos of a woman who was blinded by the makeup.

Above: Rabbits are immobilized for testing cosmetics. This test is known as the Draize test.

a substance, such as a shampoo, into the eye. Rabbits are used because they have no tear ducts that could wash away the substance.

The researcher observes the rabbits for as long as two weeks. The rabbits, meanwhile, are forced to endure what is often excruciating pain, bleeding, and blindness. Sometimes, the rabbits break their own necks in an attempt to escape.

Animal rights activists want to eliminate the Draize test, as well as other animal testing for cosmetics, because they believe it is cruel and that effective alternative tests exist. Organizations such as PETA have posted pictures of test animals with horrifying skin lesions and swollen, red eyes on websites in hopes that they would open the public's eyes to the cruelty of cosmetic testing. In this way, animal rights activists have helped to vastly reduce the use of the Draize test.

Popular opinion seems to be on their side. More and more people are demanding products that have not been tested on animals. The European Union has banned the use of animals in cosmetics tests altogether. Many individual companies around the world have taken it upon themselves to stop the testing. The words "not tested on animals" appears on countless cosmetics products, and many consumers won't buy a product that they know was developed with the use of animal testing.

Animal rights activists point out that if some companies can do this, all should follow suit. In the 1990s, several hundred companies followed the lead of the Avon company by halting all tests on animals. Pro-animal groups credit consumer boycotts against the cosmetic companies that use animals to test their products as helping to bring

Above: In 2009 PETA activists protest the use of animals for testing cosmetics and other household products.

about this change. For example, after the Animal Rights Coalition put an ad in the *New York Times* asking, "How many rabbits does Revlon blind for beauty's sake?" the company committed itself to cruelty-free cosmetics. Continued boycotts of the remaining companies that test cosmetics on animals continue in the twenty-first century.

Although the FDA still considers the Draize test an important measure of the safety of products, the popularity of the test is rapidly decreasing. Even some researchers claim the test is not effective since rabbits' eyes are not human eyes and since results seem to vary greatly from test to test. In addition, some people speculate that one researcher's visual interpretation of the degree of irritation to the rabbit may vary from another researcher's assessment.

In the twenty-first century, some researchers limit animals' exposure to chemicals, while others use computer testing instead of the Draize test. Companies can also use small portions of donated human skin or corneas to run their tests, instead of testing on animals. One animal welfare group claims that animal use for this type of testing has decreased by as much as 90 percent in recent years.

ALTERNATIVE METHODS

Proponents of the Draize test do not oppose alternatives to

> **No one wants to think of animals being used for anything other than kindness and human companionship. But it's important that we continue to recognize the risk to human health if unreliable tests are used.**
>
> —**NEIL WILCOX,** DIRECTOR OF THE FDA'S OFFICE OF ANIMAL CARE AND USE, 1995

animal testing, but they say that using alternatives is not a simple matter. The FDA requires cosmetic companies to use approved ingredients, to follow specific labeling guidelines on packages, and to test products for safety. The FDA does not specify which test should be used, meaning that cosmetic companies are self-regulated in matters related to testing. They are responsible for doing whatever is necessary to ensure the safety of a product. If an unsafe product goes on the market, the FDA will recall the product and legal action may be taken against the company.

Until recently, the Draize test has been the only test that cosmetics companies felt was valid and reliable. However, Avon has pioneered an alternative method of testing, called Eyetex, in which a synthetic material mimics the reaction of an eye. Eyetex was tested many times on more than five hundred different products before it was considered valid and reliable—a long and costly process. Even after all this testing, there is no guarantee that the result of such an alternative will be satisfactory.

Those who use the Draize test say they are doing so out of concern for human safety. Until they are 100 percent sure of alternatives, they will continue to use the Draize. They believe that it is better to risk the eyes of a rabbit than the eyes of a person.

Another alternative that companies have started to use is to place a substance on the skin, rather than the eyes, of an animal or volunteer human. If the substance irritates the skin, there is no need to proceed further.

The push for more alternative tests got real traction in the late 2000s. In 2008 three U.S. government agencies, including the National Institutes of Health, signed a "Memorandum of Understanding." It was a pact to push for and further explore tests that don't use animals, particularly in the cosmetic industry. The agencies estimated that more than 10 million animals per year were used in toxicity tests and agreed to redouble efforts to bring down that number.

Agreement Could Bring End to Animal Testing

From the Pages of USA TODAY An ambitious program announced Thursday by a coalition of government agencies could lead to the end of animal testing to evaluate the safety for humans of new chemicals and drugs.

Three agencies—the Environmental Protection Agency, the National Toxicology Program and the National Institutes of Health—have signed a "Memorandum of Understanding" to develop and implement the new methods. The collaboration is described in today's edition of the journal *Science*.

The agreement is a "milestone" says Martin Stephens of the Humane Society of the United States. "We believe this is the beginning of the end for animal testing. We think the (conversion) process will take about 10 years."

The agencies acknowledge that full implementation of the shift in toxicity testing could take years because it will require scientific validation of the new approaches.

The Humane Society and other activist groups have long protested the use of animals to test the safety of chemicals, particularly those used in cosmetics and other personal products. The agencies noted that the public's "unease" with animal testing, in addition to a growing number of new chemicals and high testing costs, fueled the new collaboration.

Although there are no actual figures, Stephens says his "best guess" would be that about 10 million animals a year are used in toxicity testing, mostly mice, rats, rabbits and guinea pigs, and then lesser numbers of dogs, monkeys and other species.

Historically, toxicity has been identified by injecting chemicals into animals and seeing whether they were harmed.

"It was expensive, time-consuming, used animals in large numbers, and it didn't always work," says Francis Collins, director of the NIH's National Human Genome Research Institute.

The new systems the agencies hope to use rely on human cells grown in test tubes and computer-driven testing machines. They allow the scientists to examine potentially toxic compounds in the lab rather than injecting them into animals.

Thousands of chemicals can be tested at one time under a method that uses a 3-by-5-inch [8 by 13 cm] glass tray with 1,536 tiny wells, each a fraction of a millimeter across, says Christopher Austin, director of NIH's Chemical Genomics Center.

A few hundred human cells grown in a test tube go into each well. Then, guided by a computer, the testing machine drips a different chemical into each well. After a while, the machine shines a laser through each well to see how many cells remain. A computer analyzes the toxicity of each compound based on how the cells react.

Above: This biochip contains human cell cultures and enzymes. The chip is designed to mimic human reactions to chemicals in toxicity studies. Many people hope the biochip will replace animal testing.

It's a wonderful example of what scientists always hope for, Collins says. "You develop a technology for one purpose, and you realize, 'Goodness! We can use it for something else!'"

—Elizabeth Weise

Countries of the European Union took things a step further. In 2009 a ban against all animal testing for cosmetics went into effect. By 2013 the European Union plans to ban the sale of all cosmetic products that have been tested on animals.

THE FIGHT AGAINST FUR

It was a cold Washington, D.C., evening on January 20, 2008, as Michelle Obama stood by the side of her husband, Barack Obama, who had earlier been sworn in as the forty-fourth president of the United States. The new First Lady

Above: Barack and Michelle Obama stand on the stage at the Home States Ball on inauguration night 2009. Animal Rights activists were pleased that the new First Lady chose not to wear fur to the inauguration or the ball.

Above: First Lady Jacqueline Kennedy *(right)* started a craze for leopard fur coats in the 1960s. Famous women such as Queen Elizabeth II *(left)* and Elizabeth Taylor *(center)* followed suit.

wore a beautiful white gown as she looked on. The gown got as much attention for what it wasn't—fur—as for what it was.

Elaborate furs used to be expected from the wife of the president. First Lady Jacqueline Kennedy once wore a fur coat made from leopard, starting a fashion that resulted in the destruction of countless leopards and almost drove the big cats to extinction. But in recent years, fur has been nowhere to be seen. From Hillary Clinton to Laura Bush to Michelle Obama, fur has become politically incorrect.

Animal rights groups applauded the First Lady's decision. These groups want to eliminate practices that they believe cause the needless suffering of animals—practices that include trapping, hunting, and raising animals for their fur. Animal rights activists view such practices as senseless and cruel. They believe that modern fabrics make it possible for people to stay warm and look good without turning to fur. Those who make their living from the fur industry and those who choose to wear fur think otherwise.

What about Leather?

While the use of leather in the fashion industry isn't as hotly contested as the use of fur, it remains a controversial subject. Leather is made from the hide of cattle. It is tough, durable, easy to shape, and considered by many to be visually appealing. Many people see no problem with leather because they believe it is a natural and useful by-product of the beef industry.

PETA and other animal rights groups are quick to point out that leather is generally not a slaughterhouse by-product. The hides of slaughtered animals typically aren't used for leather production. Instead, most leather comes from animals that are raised and slaughtered primarily for their hides. For animal rights advocates, using an animal only for fashion—and not for humansustenance— is a cruel waste of animal life.

Above: A buyer at a 2008 trade show in India examines animal skins meant for the manufacturing of leather goods.

They maintain that rais-
ing and killing animals
for their fur is an honest
and natural way to make
a living. They believe that
the choice to wear fur is a
personal one that should
be decided by individuals
and not laws.

TRAPPING FOR FUR

Around the world, more
than 10 million wild ani-
mals each year are trapped
and killed for their fur.
Animals prized for their
fur include mink, otter,
and fox. Many of them
are trapped on land by
a steel-jaw leghold trap.
This device clamps down
on the animal's legs and
immobilizes the animal
until the trapper retrieves
it. Then the animal is
killed, usually by drowning or
clubbing (methods that don't
damage the fur).

Animal rights and ani-
mal welfare groups vigorously
oppose such traps. They claim
that 25 percent of the animals
caught by these traps chew

Above: In 2001 a PETA activist holds
a fox skin in a steel trap to protest
cruelty in the fur industry.

off their own legs in a desper-
ate effort to escape. Then they
often bleed to death. Sometimes
the animals remain for days
in the traps before the trapper
retrieves them. Many of the animals caught in the traps aren't
even the ones the trappers are

seeking. Birds, deer, cats, and dogs are among the many animals that get caught and die in traps that have been set for other types of fur-bearing animals. For these reasons, many activists would like to see steel traps outlawed. Some states have done so, but trappers get around the laws by using padded traps or snares instead.

Other groups argue that trapping animals in the wild is better than the alternative of raising them on fur farms, where conditions are far bleaker. They argue that trappers are not willfully cruel. Many trappers work sixteen-hour days to retrieve animals in a timely manner so that the animals won't suffer and the furs will be in good condition. Whenever possible, trappers use traps that snap shut around the animal's neck and cause instant death. These traps are becoming more common.

Trapping is viewed by some people as an acceptable way to control wildlife populations. Some animals are trapped and killed not for their fur but to control their exploding populations in the wild. Those in favor of this type of trapping argue that overpopulated animals

How Many?

How many animals does it take to make a regular 40-inch (102 cm) fur coat? Here are the figures for a few animals popular for their furs.

Beaver: 15	Rabbit: 35
Lynx: 18	Raccoon: 40
Otter: 20	Mink: 50
Fox: 20	

compete for a limited food supply and that many suffer and die from hunger. By keeping the population in check, they argue, they are improving the lives of animals.

FUR FARMS

More than 30 million animals are bred, raised, and killed each year by fur farms. Animals at fur farms are raised for their pelts and other by-products. Mink oil, for example, is a key ingredient in many hypoallergenic cosmetics. Mink, chinchillas, and foxes make up the bulk of animals raised on fur farms.

Animal rights groups argue that conditions at fur farms are inhumane. Animals are cramped in small living quarters and exhibit stress-related behavior as a result of being confined. Some animals, for example, pace back and forth in the cages. Others don't even have room to turn around, let alone pace. For

Above: A black mink looks out of its cage at a Wisconsin fur farm.

Fetal Fur

One type of fur animal rights advocates find especially troubling is broadtail. This fur comes from unborn lambs. The mother is killed by slitting her throat. Then the unborn lamb is removed from her belly, and its skin is removed. Similar to broadtail fur is Karakul. It comes from a lamb killed just days after birth.

example, a mink on a fur farm is kept in a cage measuring about 12 by 18 inches (30 by 46 cm). By comparison, a male mink's natural range in the wild is about 2,500 acres (1,000 hectares).

Animal rights groups also argue that the animals are often deformed as a result of inbreeding (breeding animals that are genetically related, such as littermates). Further, they argue, animals are kept in exceptionally cold temperatures. The cold encourages the growth of long, thick fur but may also produce additional stress and discomfort to the animals. Animals are generally killed at a very young age, when their fur is still clean and supple. And the means of killing the animals can be exceptionally cruel. One way fur farms kill animals is by inserting a probe into the animal's anus and electrocuting it to death. This method kills the animal without doing any damage to the precious coat. Other reports indicate that animals may be skinned while still alive.

Fur farmers argue that they treat their animals humanely. After all, they say, raising the animals in a cruelty-free environment provides better-quality fur. On a mink farm, between one and four animals are housed in a 1- by 3-foot (0.3 by 1 m) enclosure. When they are ready for market, the animals are usually gassed with either carbon monoxide or carbon dioxide. The method is painless and keeps the animals' pelts clean and undamaged. Stories of crueler methods may grab headlines, but they're a rarity, fur farmers insist.

Demand for fur has dropped dramatically over the years as a result of education campaigns staged by PETA and other animal rights groups. Negative attitudes toward fur have turned it into a "fashion don't" in many circles. Young designers such as Stella McCartney (daughter of musician Paul McCartney) and Jay McCarroll, for example, have fur-free fashion lines. And many celebrities—such as Pink, Amy Smart, and Prince—are very vocal in their support of antifur campaigns. Supermodel Naomi Campbell is one celebrity known for wearing furs, and she has faced repeated public protests, many of them organized by PETA. In fact, she was once denied entry to a popular nightclub because the owner didn't believe in killing animals for their furs. Proponents of fur counter that artificial fabrics can't replicate the look and feel of fur and that wearing it is within their rights. These people believe that PETA has no right to bully people into conforming to their beliefs.

CHAPTER SIX

Animals as Entertainers

Entertainment in ancient Rome was often violent and bloody. At the Roman Colosseum, spectators watched lions, tigers, bulls, snakes, and other animals fight for their lives. For variety, slaves and soldiers were placed in the arena with the animals. They might kill the animals or be mauled and killed themselves. On other occasions, men called gladiators fought one another to the death. Onlookers cheered, as people fought one another and the animals in pools of blood. For miles around, the crowd of fifty thousand could be heard cheering for more.

In modern times, this type of sporting event involving the intentional death of humans is gruesome—and illegal. But what about when it involves animals? Is it permissible to use animals for the entertainment of humans if it causes pain and suffering to the animals?

Left: A performer and elephants from Ringling Brothers and Barnum & Bailey Circus walk through New York City in 2005. Animal rights protesters gathered along the route to campaign against the mistreatment of circus animals.

THE ABCDs OF ANIMAL ENTERTAINMENT

From parades of elephants to "man-eating" lions to dancing bears, animals have always drawn big crowds at circuses. But according to many animal rights advocates, the circus is better left to the clowns. At least they have a say in what they do.

In her book, *Thanking the Monkey: Rethinking the Way We Treat Animals*, author and animal rights activist Karen Dawn details her ABCDs of animals in entertainment. The *A* stands for acquisition. Animals in entertainment, such as elephants, must first be acquired. They are either captured from the wild or torn from their families. The *B* stands for brutality. Many entertainment venues, such as the circus, rely on punishment to teach their animals desired behaviors. In a famous video, a circus trainer is seen using a tool called a bullhook to punish an elephant in training. The trainer explains that elephants won't behave as desired unless you "hurt them, make them scream."

The *C* stands for confinement. Animals used in circuses and other entertainment venues are

Above: A former circus elephant trainer demonstrates a bullhook during a 2006 hearing about banning their use in Nebraska.

A Cruel Sport

In 2007 the arrest of National Football League (NFL) star Michael Vick brought the cruel sport of dogfighting to the public's attention. Vick was convicted of raising pit bull dogs to be used in illegal dogfights.

According to officials, Vick and his friends executed any dogs that proved to be unfit to fight or that were no longer able to fight. According to reports, they killed dogs by slamming them against walls. They also doused one dog with water and then electrocuted it to death. Vick was sentenced to twenty-three months in prison for his crimes.

Many of Vick's dogs were sent to a shelter for rehabilitation. The staff of the shelter helped them heal and worked with them to make them safe for adoption. Over more than a year, most of the dogs responded to the attention—even some that had been considered too badly abused to ever be adoptable. Many of them have since gone to good homes as family pets. Others were unable to recover and will spend the rest of their lives at the shelter.

often caged in unnatural enclosures that are far too small for them. Finally, *D* stands for disposal. What becomes of animals when they're too old or otherwise unable to provide entertainment? The animals may be pawned off on a zoo or rescue shelter or simply killed. Put it all together, animal rights activists say, and it's not a pretty picture. Should any animal be subjected to this kind of life simply for the purposes of entertainment?

The problem isn't unique to the circus. Large aquariums keep dolphins, whales, seals, and other marine mammals to perform for crowds. Bullfighting arenas keep bulls to be tormented and often killed for the entertainment of the crowd. Dawn's ABCDs apply to these places as well. They also apply to zoos, rodeos, racetracks for dogs and horses, and countless other venues where animals are the center of entertainment.

PETA Activists Want to See Change after Fatal Trip

From the Pages of
USA TODAY

Ingrid Newkirk, president of People for the Ethical Treatment of Animals (PETA), proposed far-reaching changes in Thoroughbred racing Monday after the death of the filly Eight Belles in the Kentucky Derby [the horse was put down immediately after breaking both of her ankles during the race].

Newkirk, in a letter to the Kentucky Horse Racing Authority (KHRA), urged regulations that were described as a "bare minimum for horse safety."

- Thoroughbreds under the age of 3 should not be permitted to race.
- Synthetic surfaces or turf—which result in fewer injuries—should be mandated at all race courses.
- Whipping should be banned.

PETA, which plans to demonstrate at the Kentucky Horse Racing Authority's Lexington, Kentucky, headquarters today, also urged the suspension of jockey Gabriel Saez for what it viewed as excessive whipping of Eight Belles on Saturday that it thought was "clearly pushing her beyond her physical limits."

The KHRA responded with a statement citing the absence of scientific evidence to suggest that any of the first three changes would enhance the safety of equine [horse-riding] athletes.

It described the whip as a tool that "provides safety for all participants" and noted that abuse of the whip constitutes a violation of Kentucky racing regulations.

Above: Eight Belles and her trainer prepare for the Kentucky Derby on May 3, 2008.

Above: Eight Belles collapsed on the track after breaking both her legs while cooling down after the Kentucky Derby in 2008.

The KHRA concluded its statement by saying, "Kentucky stewards reviewed videotapes of the Derby and saw no evidence of a violation of any racing regulation by Mr. Gabriel Saez during the course of the race."

Saez, 20, declined interview requests. He issued a statement through Delaware Park: "I remain heartbroken over Eight Belles, and I want to let her many fans know that she never gave me the slightest indication before or during the race that there was anything bothering her. All I could sense under me was how eager she was to race. I was so proud of her performance and of the opportunity to ride her in my first Kentucky Derby, all of which adds to my sadness."

Former jockey Chris McCarron, a two-time Derby winner and now an analyst for TVG racing network, said, "Jockeys don't make horses break down. There is nothing you can do to cause injury unless you are really reckless."

McCarron said of PETA's proposals: "It's not going to change the game because these particular changes and suggestions just do not have merit. For the most part, race horses are very well cared for."

Newkirk is adamant that an overhaul must occur, saying in the news release issued by PETA, "Compassionate people will not continue to tolerate a dirty sport in which animals are ridden [to] death."

—Tom Pedulla

People who use animals in the entertainment business insist that cruelty is the exception, not the rule. They point out that anti-cruelty laws exist to protect animals from harsh treatment. They claim that the public would never support an act that was based around cruelty to animals. They also argue that their displays are a great way to educate people about animals. As the public learns to appreciate animals, the animals' interests will be better served. Perhaps the best example of the debate about animals in entertainment is in the arena of modern zoos.

ZOOS: EDUCATION OR ENTERTAINMENT?

For many people, zoos provide entertainment and education. Many large, well-established zoos in the United States strive to be accredited by the Association of Zoos and Aquariums (AZA). Wildlife conservation is one of the main purposes of accredited zoos. Breeding animals in captivity may offer the only means of survival for many species that face extinction in nature. Zookeepers take care of the animals' needs. Most zoos employ zoologists (also called curators) and veterinarians as well. Accredited zoos also provide educational programs and tours and entertainment for visitors of all ages.

The trend among larger zoos is to provide the animals with more spacious, natural environments. For example, at the Bronx Zoo's Jungle World in New York City, sounds of jungle insects and birds are broadcasted through speakers to give the zoo's animals—as well as its visitors—a feeling of being in the wild. At the San Diego Zoo's Wild Animal Park in California, more than two thousand wild animals roam free on 700 acres (283 hectares) of land that resemble their native African habitat. People who visit the exhibit view the animals from inside the monorail car that moves quietly across the zoo's landscape.

Zoo supporters point out another benefit of natural habitats. Animals are more likely to mate in these environments, thus promoting survival of their species. A rhino at the San Diego Zoo that had never mated in a confined zoo has fathered fifty-five offspring since being moved to an open environment. In more organized efforts, some zoos have captive breeding programs. These programs assist the animals in mating and, in some cases, returning the young to the wild, where their species can live and breed naturally. Israel and Jordan, for example, have received rare antelope from the San Diego Zoo. And the Bronx Zoo has returned condors to the wild. Without such programs, many species would face a greater danger of extinction.

THE ARGUMENT AGAINST ZOOS

Critics do not agree that all "natural" zoos are good for animals. Often animal enclosures are built to look natural, but it's only an illusion for the sake of the public. For example, the gorilla enclosure at the Buffalo Zoo in New York went through a $1 million renovation that featured natural trees and plants.

Below: Mother and daughter Indian rhinoceroses have room to wander around the open environment at the San Diego Zoo's Wild Animal Park in California.

Maggie's Plight

The Alaska Zoo in Anchorage, Alaska, had been Maggie's home for more than twenty years. Maggie was the zoo's only elephant. Elephants are very social creatures, needing the company of other elephants, but Maggie was alone. She spent Alaska's long winters by herself in a barn. She had no companionship, little exercise, and her health was suffering.

In response to complaints, the zoo tried to build Maggie a sort of treadmill. But it did no good. Several times, Maggie lay down and lacked the strength to stand back up again. Finally, public criticism forced the zoo to give up Maggie. The elephant was sent to a sanctuary in California. There, Maggie had wide-open spaces to roam. And more important, she had the company of others of her kind. Her health quickly rebounded, and she is living a healthier and happier life in California.

Above: Maggie eats snow in her pen at the Alaska Zoo in Anchorage before being moved to a sanctuary in California.

> ❝ **How do you, on the one hand, try to make the elephants live a better life and at the same time enable young children and future generations to have enough exposure to them in order to develop an affection and an appreciation and an understanding of these animals?** ❞
>
> **—JOHN KAY,** ELEPHANT ACTIVIST,
> ON THE USE OF ELEPHANTS IN ENTERTAINMENT
> **USA TODAY · JUNE 3, 2005**

But while it may have looked great from the outside, the animals weren't really free to enjoy it inside. They were fenced off from the natural elements inside the enclosure.

Animal welfare advocates point out that in some cases, captivity seems to lessen not only the quality of an animal's life but also its life expectancy. A 2008 study showed that African elephants living in Kenya's Amboseli National Park lived, on average, fifty-six years. African elephants living in zoos, meanwhile, lived an average of just seventeen years. The trend held true for Asian elephants as well.

Additionally, critics of zoos claim that breeding animals in zoos is a dangerous business. Surplus animals (those not needed by the zoos) are sometimes sold to animal entertainment shows, and sometimes they must be destroyed—why?

WILL THE SHOW GO ON?

The most radical animal rights groups would like animals in entertainment banned altogether. Circuses can be just as entertaining without animals, a theory tested and proved by the popular "animal-free" French Canadian circus Cirque du Soleil. Animal rights activists will continue to hold public protests and to lobby for legislation to see that rodeos, whale shows, and other forms of animal entertainment become things of the past.

In 2008 the ASPCA, along with other animal rights groups, sued the Ringling Brothers and Barnum & Bailey Circus. The lawsuit claimed that the circus's animals—in particular the elephants—were subject to cruel and inhumane treatment. The animal rights groups argued that the elephants were kept in cramped quarters, abused with clubs and bullhooks, and suffered other abuses. Circus representatives contended that the animals had veterinary care around the clock and that they were well cared for. The case went to court in early 2009. While the ASPCA and animal groups insist that their goal is to eliminate abuse, not to ban animal entertainers outright, the result will likely play a big role in the future of animals in the circus.

In general, however, the public seems to be in favor of using animals as entertainers, as long as it is done without cruelty. Attractions such as San Diego's SeaWorld attract millions of paying visitors each year. These visitors enjoy watching the

Below: A trainer poses with a killer whale at SeaWorld in San Diego. Many people visit SeaWorld each year. Public opinion favors animals as entertainers in cruelty-free environments.

animals—sometimes performing and sometimes in a natural habitat—and they want to continue to have that opportunity. As long as that's true, it seems that the show will go on.

PETS

In recent decades, the practice of keeping animals as pets has become controversial. Do we have the right to keep animals? Even the term *pet* itself is questioned—many prefer the term *companion animal*. While some pets, such as dogs and house cats, have been bred for thousands of years to live with us, many other types of pets are little more than wild animals in cages. For example, birds, reptiles, fish, and many other animals aren't born to live in cages, animal rights activists argue. Many such pets live in small cages or aquariums. Imagine life as a goldfish, swimming alone endlessly in a tiny bowl. Do we have the right to collect and keep such animals? And some wild animals can become a danger to their owners and other people around them. A tiger cub might seem cute, but it will grow up to become a powerful wild animal. Keeping such an animal as a pet may be a huge danger, as well as a disservice to the animal.

Few people argue against keeping cats and dogs as pets. But many people point to the inhumane ways in which many pets are bred, raised, and sold. Take the case of a pet store. Who can resist stopping to watch the

USA TODAY Snapshots®

The pet story

Total number of pets owned in the USA (in millions):

Fish — 148.6

Cats — 90.5

Dogs — 73.9

Small animals — 18.2

Birds — 16.6

Reptiles — 11

Source: American Pet Product Manufacturers Association

By David Stuckey and Marcy E. Mullins, USA TODAY, 2007

puppies through a pet store window? But where do these puppies come from? In some cases, they come from responsible breeders. But in many cases, they come from large commercial breeding operations, often called puppy mills. The dogs used to breed these puppies are kept in unhealthy, harmful conditions. They're caged, often forced to live in their own waste, and receive little exercise or affection. Their only purpose is to breed so that the owners can sell the puppies—often highly desirable purebred breeds—to pet stores and pet owners. And when dogs are no longer useful for breeding, they are destroyed.

Instead of going to an animal shelter to adopt a dog or cat in need of a home, many owners want a puppy or kitten from a breeder or a pet store. They may want a specific breed or the assurance that the animal is a pure breed. They argue that purebred animals are more predictable than mutts (mixed breeds). For example, a purebred black lab is likely to be a better hunting dog than a mutt.

Above: Many puppy mill owners take very little care of the animals they use for breeding.

Cloning Fluffy?

The loss of a pet can be devastating to many owners. That's why some pet owners have begun to explore the possibility of cloning their beloved pets. In 2002 researchers at Texas A&M University announced the first cloned cat, named CC (short for Copy Cat). Two years later, the first animal cloned to replace a pet was created in the United States, a kitten named Little Nicky. The pet owner, saddened by the death of her seventeen-year-old cat, paid a reported fifty thousand dollars for the cloned animal.

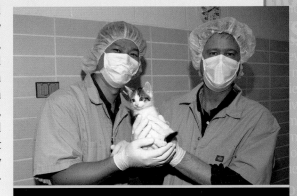

Above: Dr. Tai Young *(left)* and Dr. Mark Westhusin, the researchers who first cloned a cat, hold CC six weeks after she was born in 2002.

In 2005 South Korean scientists did successfully clone a dog—an Afghan hound named Snuppy. Since then more and more pet owners have investigated the possibility. Many are merely storing genetic material, in hopes the cost of cloning comes down. Others don't care about the cost. A U.S. woman reportedly paid a South Korean company $150,000 in 2008 to clone her beloved pit bull, Booger.

Is it right to clone a pet? Owners can get an exact genetic copy of their pet, but that doesn't make it the same animal. None of the animal's experiences or memories survives. Owning a cloned animal is more like owning the twin of an animal—the genetics might be the same, but the personality of the animal depends on its environment as well. Wouldn't the money spent on cloned pets be better put toward solving the pet overpopulation problem? Or is any cost worth it to bring back some small part of a lost pet?

Meanwhile, overpopulation of dogs and cats is a major concern across the country. As one way of dealing with the problem, humane societies and animal shelters put to death millions of unwanted dogs and cats every year. Many are mutts, unpopular breeds, or overbred breeds that shelters are unable to adopt out. Others have been abandoned by their owners.

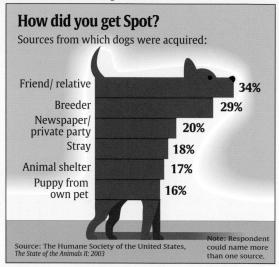

USA TODAY Snapshots®

How did you get Spot?

Sources from which dogs were acquired:

Friend/ relative **34%**
Breeder **29%**
Newspaper/ private party **20%**
Stray **18%**
Animal shelter **17%**
Puppy from own pet **16%**

Note: Respondent could name more than one source.

Source: The Humane Society of the United States, *The State of the Animals II: 2003*

By David Stuckey and Sam Ward, USA TODAY, 2006

Many humane societies have begun to routinely spay and neuter animals before offering them for adoption. These surgeries prevent

> " As long as there's a market for their [puppies], dogs will continue to be bred, neglected, and killed at puppy mills. . . . If you adopt an animal from the shelter, you'll not only save her life, you'll also help end the suffering of countless dogs at puppy mills. "

—**CHARLIZE THERON,** ACTRESS AND PETA MEMBER, 2008

Above: These dogs are waiting to be adopted from a Texas animal shelter.

the animals from breeding and creating more unwanted dogs or cats. Other shelters offer low-cost spaying or neutering of animals before they can be adopted. Some shelters require people to sign an agreement to spay or neuter pets before they can be adopted. Other humane societies conduct in-depth interviews with those interested in adopting an animal to educate them about the serious responsibilities of owning a companion animal. Studies show that a single unspayed female cat can lead to more than four hundred thousand descendants within just seven years. Most people on both sides of this debate agree that pet owners should have their animals spayed or neutered. It's a rare bit of common ground on a complex and emotional debate.

CHAPTER SEVEN

Animals and Industry

ALASKA IS A LAND RICH WITH NATURAL BEAUTY, AS well as with natural resources. Sometimes, these two features clash. That was the case with the Arctic National Wildlife Refuge (ANWR) in northeastern Alaska. The wildlife refuge is home to more than one hundred thousand caribou, as well as other arctic wildlife. But ANWR's Coastal Plain has drawn interest for a very different reason—oil.

As the United States' dependence on foreign oil has grown and prices have soared, many politicians have called for a greater focus on producing oil domestically. The United States is not, however, blessed with many huge oil reserves. ANWR is one place where drilling could make a difference, say proponents. According to some, drilling in ANWR could supply the nation with more than a million barrels of oil per day. But because the refuge is protected from industrial development, the oil sits untapped.

Left: A herd of Porcupine caribou migrates across the Arctic National Wildlife Refuge in Alaska. Many people want to explore ANWR for oil, but others are worried about the effect it will have on wildlife.

Obstacle to Drilling for Oil in ANWR is Removed; Senate Gains Vote for Plan

From the Pages of USA TODAY A controversial plan to allow oil drilling in Alaska's Arctic National Wildlife Refuge is likely to move forward now that there will be enough votes in the Senate to push the measure ahead.

When the new Congress meets in January, the Senate will have three more members than it does now who favor opening the refuge to energy exploration. The Senate has been the last significant obstacle to drilling approval.

Environmentalists say drilling in the refuge would despoil one of the USA's last pristine wildernesses, a place where caribou and wolves roam. Industry groups and Alaskan politicians say the refuge holds enough oil—the source of gasoline—to lessen U.S. dependence on foreign supplies from places like Iraq.

Both Democratic and Republican leaders say that as a result of the Nov. 2 elections, the Senate will almost certainly muster the votes to overturn the existing ban on ANWR drilling. That vote could come as early as April. President Bush and the House of Representatives have long favored drilling.

"The votes are just not there to defeat it," says Sen. Jeff Bingaman of New Mexico, senior Democrat on the energy committee and a longtime foe of drilling in the refuge.

The resignation of Energy Secretary Spencer Abraham, announced Monday, is not likely to affect the drilling debate. He supported drilling in the refuge, and whoever succeeds him will probably share that opinion.

"The administration's position is that we need to develop more domestic [energy] sources, including the proven oil reserves in Alaska," says Jeanne Lopatto, an Energy Department spokeswoman.

The Senate has been environmentalists' best hope for preventing development of the refuge. But if the Senate overturns the drilling ban, opponents say they would take the matter to court.

Democrats say supporters are likely to attach a pro-drilling provision to a budget resolution or reconciliation bill next spring. They tried to do so in 2003, but the provision was killed by a vote of 52–48.

The Senate still has enough Democrats to use the stalling technique of a filibuster, which takes 60 votes to overturn. But Senate rules prevent using a filibuster on budget resolution and reconciliation bills, says Bill Wicker, a spokesman for the Democratic members of the Senate energy committee.

Oil companies don't openly express enthusiasm for starting work in the refuge.

"We'll evaluate that opportunity and assess it against other exploration opportunities . . . and then we'll decide," says Daren Beaudo of oil giant BP.

But companies have good reason not to appear eager to dive into the refuge, says Michael Rodgers of PFC Energy, an energy consulting firm.

"I don't think companies can benefit from getting in the middle of this right now," he says. "Whenever it's possible for them to get their hands on significant reserves, they're very interested."

The nation has been fighting about the refuge for more than 20 years. Passions and rhetoric have often been intense. In 2001, House Majority Leader Tom DeLay, R-Texas, said a pro-drilling vote would "crack the backs of radical environmentalists."

Of the 52 senators who voted in 2003 to protect the refuge from development, four are being replaced by people who favor drilling. Only one senator who favored drilling is being replaced.

By one federal estimate, the refuge holds more than 4 billion barrels of oil ready for the taking. The USA consumes roughly 20 million barrels of oil a day.

Environmentalists and energy companies alike think allowing drilling in the Arctic refuge could make it easier to open other protected areas to oil exploration.

—Traci Watson and Tom Kenworthy

> " **Energy development is quite compatible with the protection of our wildlife and their habitat. For example, North Slope caribou herds have grown and remained healthy throughout more than three decades of our oil development.** "
>
> —**SARAH PALIN,** GOVERNOR OF ALASKA AND FORMER VICE-PRESIDENTIAL CANDIDATE, ON THE DEBATE OVER ANWR DRILLING, 2009

Opponents of drilling in ANWR claim that the amount of oil there isn't enough to warrant the potential damage to the environment and wildlife that call ANWR home. The battle over whether to use the protected land for oil drilling became a central piece of the presidential elections of both 2004 and 2008. It is a battle that has been fought for years and likely will be for a long time.

STRIKING THE BALANCE

The balance between wildlife, the environment, and industry has been a subject of controversy for decades. Perhaps no situation better defines the debate than the case of the spotted owl in the Pacific Northwest. This area is known for its wide expanses of forest and the logging industry that thrives there. In 1990 controversy erupted in the Pacific Northwest, and the cause was the plight of the spotted owl.

The spotted owl stands about 18 inches (45 cm) high, is dark brown with white spots, and has large eyes. In the 1800s, approximately seventeen hundred pairs of owls lived among the trees of the Pacific Northwest. By 1990 the number had dropped to half that. Environmentalists and animal rights groups feared that the spotted owl would become extinct if its habitat continued to shrink. Many biologists and wildlife experts blamed the lumber industry for the drop in the owl population. But the federal government was selling the land to lumber companies, which cut down the trees.

The cutting down of forests may have been bad for wildlife, but it was an economic boon for the people of the area. Thousands of people's jobs depended on the logging effort, and to many, the fate of a small owl didn't seem like a big deal by comparison.

In 1990 conservationists called for the U.S. Fish and Wildlife Service, another federal agency, to place the spotted owl on the endangered species list. According to U.S. policy, measures would then have to be taken to protect the owl that would mean a halt to logging in some areas of the forest. The lumber industry objected to the proposal and claimed that such a measure would result in a massive loss of jobs.

In late June, the U.S. Fish and Wildlife Service placed the spotted owl on the endangered species list. In the end, more than 2.4 million acres (1 million hectares) in the state of Washington were set aside. They were off limits to the logging companies. As predicted, the move cost about thirty thousand jobs. Almost twenty years later, the spotted owl remains on the endangered species list. Its numbers do not appear to be rebounding, and the forest remains off limits to loggers.

The spotted owl controversy is just one example of much bigger questions in the debate about animal rights. Should a product or an industry be limited when the survival of a species is at stake? And should wildlife be preserved even when preservation causes economic hardship, such as the loss of jobs, to people?

IS CONSERVATION OF WILDLIFE NECESSARY?

Not all scientists believe in conservation. Some believe extinction is a normal part of evolution—a theory based on the rule of the survival of the fittest.

Species on Endangered List Challenged; Tables Turned as Industry Groups File More Suits

From the Pages of USA TODAY

Ever since a 3-inch [8 cm] fish protected by the Endangered Species Act stopped construction of a dam in Tennessee in 1978, the law has been known as one of the toughest environmental laws on the books.

Environmental groups have used it to halt development in pristine lands across the nation. Today, the law designed to protect animals such as the manatee from extinction also has become a legal tool of property rights groups and developers.

In a counterpunch to environmentalists who have filed lawsuits aimed at protecting hundreds of plant and animal species by listing them as endangered or threatened, property rights groups such as the Pacific Legal Foundation are filing lawsuits to have animals and plants removed from the list so that development can proceed.

Meanwhile, industry groups have filed dozens of legal challenges aimed at allowing development on lands set aside by the U.S. government to help protect endangered species.

"The conventional wisdom is that environmental groups exclusively used this provision in court, but today, the industry lawsuits challenging critical habitat designations far outnumber environmental challenges," says Pat Parenteau, a law professor at Vermont Law School in South Royalton, Vt.

In a study he published last August on active litigation involving the Endangered Species Act, Parenteau counted 45 lawsuits filed by industry groups and five filed by environmental groups.

At the forefront of the movement is the National Association of Home Builders, which recently prevailed in a legal battle over Arizona land that had been designated as a habitat for the cactus ferruginous pygmy owl. Two environmental groups have sued to restore the designation, and a court hearing on the issue is scheduled for Friday.

Likewise, the conservative Pacific Legal Foundation, based in Sacramento [California], is pressing the federal government to re-examine several animals and plants on the endangered list.

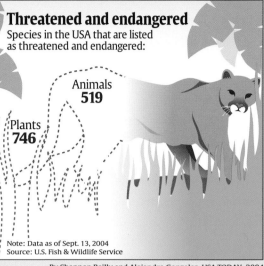

USA TODAY Snapshots

Threatened and endangered

Species in the USA that are listed as threatened and endangered:

Plants
746

Animals
519

Note: Data as of Sept. 13, 2004
Source: U.S. Fish & Wildlife Service

By Shannon Reilly and Alejandro Gonzalez, USA TODAY, 2004

Both groups have found a relatively friendly audience in the Bush administration, which in recent years has loosened many of the restrictions in the Endangered Species Act. Among other things, the administration has focused on giving private property owners incentives to protect vulnerable species, rather than banning activity on their land.

"We've had property owners coming to us for years," says Rob Rivett, chief attorney for the foundation. "Finally, it became clear we didn't have any choice but to try to balance the scales."

Most of the legal battles over the Endangered Species Act are taking place in rapidly growing urban areas in the South and West.

In the Tucson fight over the cactus ferruginous pygmy owl, The National Association of Home Builders objected to the government's plan to set aside 1.2 million acres [0.5 hectares] for the animal and fought to have it removed from the endangered species list. Last month, the Bush administration announced it would take the owl off the list.

That decision prompted two environmental groups to sue in Tucson federal court to block the delisting, says Kieran Suckling, policy director for the Center for Biological Diversity.

—Laura Parker

According to this theory, animals that cannot quickly adapt to a changing environment will die out. More adaptable species, such as squirrels and cockroaches, manage to thrive even in city landscapes. Evolutionists say that while humans happen to be dominant at this point in time, we may be replaced in thousands of years to come if we can't adjust to changing environmental conditions. Some go so far as to say that it is unnatural to make a special effort to save weaker species.

Conservationists reply that the kind of extinction taking place in the industrial era is anything but natural. Reports on how many species disappear per year vary widely by source,

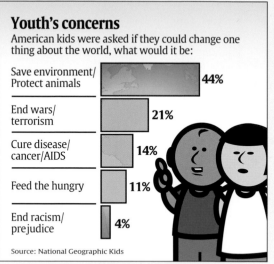

USA TODAY Snapshots®

Youth's concerns
American kids were asked if they could change one thing about the world, what would it be:

Save environment/Protect animals — **44%**

End wars/terrorism — **21%**

Cure disease/cancer/AIDS — **14%**

Feed the hungry — **11%**

End racism/prejudice — **4%**

Source: National Geographic Kids

By David Stuckey and Keith Simmons, USA TODAY, 2008

but the number could be as high as twenty-seven thousand per year. Another estimate says that extinction rates are magnified up to one thousand times over historic rates due to human activity. In a simpler example, a recent report indicates that at current rates, 12 percent of

> " **We can use [our power over animals] to be cruel and indifferent, or to be kind and careful stewards.** "

—**DAVID MARTOSKO,** DIRECTOR OF RESEARCH
FOR THE CENTER FOR CONSUMER FREEDOM

USA TODAY · JANUARY 28, 2008

Saving the Whales

One issue that commonly unites animal rights groups and environmentalists is the protection of marine mammals, especially whales. These highly intelligent mammals were once hunted worldwide for their meat and oil. But a worldwide ban on whaling, passed in 1986, has significantly dropped the number of whales killed each year. In 1986 more than six thousand whales were killed by whalers. That number dropped to under six hundred by 1992, before it started climbing again. By the turn of the century, it was back up to about fifteen hundred whales per year.

Only a few countries still allow whaling, including Norway and Japan. Ships full of protesters often take to the ocean to try to save whales from their hunters. Protesters place their small ships and boats between whales and whaling ships, often leading to violent clashes between whalers and protesters.

all known bird species will be extinct by the end of the twenty-first century.

The balance between industry and the environment is difficult to strike. The presence of industry often leads to pollution and the destruction of natural habitats. It can contribute to the suffering of animals and even to extinctions. But Earth's human population is growing, and its needs are increasing. Industry means more homes, jobs, food, and cars. Under these circumstances, should the needs of human beings come first? Or should the needs of animals and humans be balanced? Communities struggle to make these decisions as the human population grows and the demand for opening new lands increases each year.

CHAPTER EIGHT

Today and Tomorrow

IN SOME WAYS, ANIMAL RIGHTS ACTIVISTS WOULD like to fundamentally change the culture of U.S. society. What we eat, what we wear, and how we look at ourselves in relation to the environment are at issue. What can we expect in the years to come? Animal rights groups such as PETA will probably continue to organize demonstrations and creative advertising campaigns against those whom they consider to be violators of animal rights. PETA plans to use consumer support to persuade industries to operate in a cruelty-free manner. With the help of citizens, it hopes to push pro-animal laws through state and federal governments.

Other groups, such as ALF and the closely related Earth Liberation Front (ELF), will likely grab headlines in a less traditional manner. Whether the extreme actions of such groups hurt or help the cause for animal rights is unclear. While acts of violence and intimidation certainly make headlines and put animal rights issues in

Left: A shopper buys meat at a deli in a grocery store in Maryland. The animal rights debate has an impact on what people eat and wear.

Animal Rights Fight Gains Momentum

From the Pages of
USA TODAY
The growing influence of animal rights activists increasingly is affecting daily life, touching everything from the foods Americans eat to what they study in law school, where they buy their puppies and even whether they should enjoy a horse-drawn carriage ride in New York's Central Park.

Animal activist groups such as the Humane Society of the United States and People for the Ethical Treatment of Animals (PETA) say they are seeing a spike in membership as their campaigns spread.

"There's been an explosion of interest" in animal welfare issues, says David Favre, a Michigan State University law professor and animal law specialist. "Groups like the Humane Society of the United States and PETA have brought to our social awareness their concerns about animals and all matter of creatures."

"Animals are made of flesh and blood and bone, just like humans," says Bruce Friedrich, PETA's vice president for campaigns. "They feel pain just like we do. Recognition of that grows year by year. The animal rights movement is a social justice movement [similar to] suffrage [voting] and civil rights."

Among other initiatives, PETA supports a measure introduced last month by a New York City councilman that would ban carriage horses that haul tourists around Manhattan. Many other cities feature such businesses.

"I think it's clear that animal issues are part of the public domain the news, they may also push people away from animal rights causes by being too extreme. ALF is one of a handful of animal rights groups considered to be a terrorist organization under the United States' Patriot Act of 2001. And in 2006, the U.S. Congress passed the Animal Enterprise Terrorism Act specifically to target such groups.

Still, membership among animal rights groups is booming. PETA's membership alone like never before," says Michael Markarian, executive vice president of the Humane Society, the largest animal welfare organization. "People have started thinking more and more about how we treat animals in our society."

Food producers say the activists aren't just concerned about animal welfare but are trying to win them the same rights as human beings.

"Ultimately, their goal is to eliminate animals being used as food," says Kay Johnson-Smith of the Animal Agriculture Alliance, an industry-supported organization that seeks to educate the public about agriculture. "There's a real danger when we allow a very small minority of activists to dictate procedures that should be used to raise animals for food."

David Martosko, director of research for the Center for Consumer Freedom, an organization supported by restaurants and food companies, says most Americans oppose cruelty to animals. But he says that activists who say animals shouldn't be eaten or used for medical research or any other purpose won't find much mainstream support.

"That is a position that very few Americans agree with," he says.

Martosko also says abandoning some current agricultural practices will drive up food prices. According to the American Farm Bureau Federation, a dozen regular eggs cost $1.56 in mid-2007, compared with $2.89 for cage-free eggs.

Janet Riley, senior vice president of public affairs for the American Meat Institute, whose members produce about 95% of the beef, pork, lamb, veal and turkey consumed in the USA, says the industry is diligent in handling animals humanely. But, she adds, "people have different opinions about what constitutes humane handling."

—Larry Copeland

has tripled since the 1980s. And the push for healthier eating, smaller producers raising and selling animals locally, and restaurants based on buying from local producers is on the increase across the United States. From their successes in dramatically reducing the demand for fur to the raising of awareness of conditions for animals on factory farms and in slaughterhouses, the push for animal rights has gained momentum.

THE GROWING OPPOSITION

Meanwhile, opponents of animal rights groups have been mounting their own campaigns. The Congressional Animal Welfare Caucus is a group of U.S. members of Congress that supports the use of animals in medical research. Organizations such as the American Medical Association have come out in favor of animal testing. Some groups have gone so far as to label animal rights groups "anti-science." The

What Can You Do?

Is animal welfare an issue that concerns you? If so, how can you act on your feelings? With a few simple steps, you can make a difference:

- Don't buy cosmetics or shampoos unless they're not tested on animals. Most products not tested on animals will say so on the packaging somewhere. If there's a product you like but are unsure of, call the manufacturer to get the facts.
- Choose synthetic fabrics over fur or leather. Or choose natural fibers such as cotton and wool, which are long wearing, comfortable, and fashionable but do not rely on the death of an animal.
- Reduce the amount of meat you eat, or look for meat and eggs labeled "free range."
- Eat at restaurants that offer animal products (eggs, meat, cheese, etc.) that are produced locally and raised on free-range farms.
- Choose vegetarian meals at your local fast-food restaurant.
- If your science class is planning to dissect an animal, ask if you can choose not to participate due to your beliefs. If

actions of animal rights groups have been portrayed as violent and a threat to public choice.

Meanwhile, organizations such as iiFAR and the Foundation for Biomedical Research run their own public relations campaigns, touting the benefits of using animals in research. Other grassroots groups, such as Putting People First (PPF) do their part to present the other side of the debate at animal rights demonstrations.

the teacher refuses, take the issue to the principal or the school board.

- If you and your family are getting a pet, choose a pet from your local humane society or animal shelter instead of from a pet store, purebred breeder, or puppy mill.
- Talk to your friends and family about animal rights. You might get them thinking along the same lines you are.
- Write a letter to your state representative or senator to express your concerns about animal rights and to seek support on this issue.

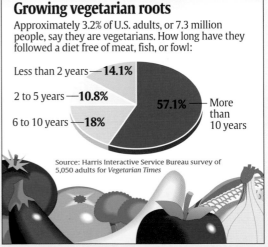

USA TODAY Snapshots®

Growing vegetarian roots

Approximately 3.2% of U.S. adults, or 7.3 million people, say they are vegetarians. How long have they followed a diet free of meat, fish, or fowl:

Less than 2 years — **14.1%**

2 to 5 years — **10.8%**

6 to 10 years — **18%**

57.1% — More than 10 years

Source: Harris Interactive Service Bureau survey of 5,050 adults for *Vegetarian Times*

By Michelle Healy and Keith Simmons, USA TODAY, 2008

The battle wages on both in the public eye as well as in the halls of government. Powerful lobbies on both sides of the issue press lawmakers for support. The result is often long, expensive, drawn-out battles in which neither side clearly wins. The animal rights movement has made significant progress over the past one hundred years. Protection exists for many farm animals, some laboratory animals, animals in slaughterhouses, and more. Vegetarianism and veganism are on the rise. Surveys indicate that 2 percent or more of Americans do not eat meat. Among young people ages eight to eighteen, the figure is about 3 percent.

WHAT ARE THE CHANCES FOR CHANGE?

Think of all the world's problems in the 2000s, from unrest in the Middle East to climate change to the perilous state of the worldwide economy. A skeptic might say that in such a stressful political climate, the plight of animals will be forgotten. In a world of limited resources, many people

> " **What if we drop all this talk of rights and instead advocate a sense of obligation? In the same way that we teach children to respect a tree by mentioning its age, we should use the new insights into animals' mental life to foster in humans an ethic of caring in which our interests are not the only ones in the balance.** "

—**FRANS DE WAAL,**
PRIMATOLOGIST, 2009

> " We need to recognize at the outset that what we do to animals from their perspective certainly, and probably from ours, is morally wrong and unacceptable. "

—**JANE GOODALL,** PRIMATOLOGIST

USA TODAY · MAY 28, 2008

think that the human suffering caused by war, poverty, hunger, and homelessness should take precedence over concern for animals.

Animal rights activists, on the other hand, suggest that there could be no better time than the present to examine our values and our position in the world in relation to all living things. Perhaps, they say, people will use the crises in the modern world as an opportunity for change—change in which humans will respect animals as part of an overall philosophy of caring for Earth and all its precious resources on which we depend.

TIMELINE

300s B.C. Greek philosopher Aristotle reasons that humans have dominion over animals.

A.D. 1600s French philosopher René Descartes believes that animals do not have souls or consciousness and therefore are merely machines, incapable of thought.

1700s The question of animal welfare grows more prominent with the writings of European writers and philosophers such as Voltaire and Jeremy Bentham.

1796 British doctor Edward Jenner introduces the first effective smallpox vaccine. He used both human and animal testing to develop it.

1822 The British Parliament passes an anticruelty law to protect work animals from abuse.

1840 Great Britain's Royal Society for the Prevention of Cruelty to Animals forms.

1859 Charles Darwin publishes his theory of evolution in a book titled *On the Origin of Species*, causing many to reconsider the relationship between human beings and animals.

1866 The American Society for the Prevention of Cruelty to Animals (ASPCA) forms.

1871 Darwin publishes *The Descent of Man*, in which he directly places human beings in the same evolutionary chain as animals.

1873 The U.S. Congress passes the 28-Hour Law, requiring animals being transported by train to a slaughterhouse to be given food and water at least every twenty-eight hours.

1906 Congress passes the Pure Food and Drug Act, which helps to regulate conditions in slaughterhouses.

1938   After the drug Elixir Sulfanilamide kills one hundred people, Congress passes the Federal Food, Drug, and Cosmetic Act of 1938, requiring animal testing to prove products safe.

1955   Jonas Salk announces his polio vaccine, developed with the help of animal testing.

1958   Congress passes the Humane Slaughter Act. It requires animals at slaughterhouses to be stunned before they are put to death.

1966   Congress passes the Animal Welfare Act. It offers basic protection to many species of laboratory animals.

1976   The Animal Liberation Front (ALF) forms in the United Kingdom.

1980   Alex Pacheco and Ingrid Newkirk found the group People for the Ethical Treatment of Animals (PETA).

1984   Doctors successfully transplant a heart from a baboon to a human, known as Baby Fae. This is the world's first animal-to-human transplant. Baby Fae dies three weeks after the transplant.

1985   ALF releases stolen videotapes showing horrors inflicted on animals during medical research.

The group Incurably Ill for Animal Research forms, supporting the use of animals in medical research.

1989   The Avon cosmetics company stops all animal testing on its products.

1990   Controversy erupts in the Pacific Northwest over logging rights and the endangered spotted owl. Ultimately, the government declares more than 2.4 million acres (1 million hectares) of land off limits to logging companies.

A worldwide ban on the trading of ivory goes into effect.

1992 The United Nations drafts a resolution to end all large-scale drift-net fishing.

1993 The Great Ape Project is founded to seek greater rights and protection for the great apes.

1997 Scientists successfully clone a sheep, named Dolly—the world's first cloned animal.

1998 A Humane Society investigation reveals that a U.S. retailer has been selling fur coats made with cat and dog fur.

2006 The USDA updates the 28-Hour Law to include animals transported by truck.

2007 National Football League star Michael Vick is arrested on charges of animal cruelty for taking part in an illegal dogfighting ring.

2008 PETA's membership grows to more than 1.8 million. Racehorse Eight Belles is put down after a fall at the Kentucky Derby irreparably damages both of her front legs.

An Austrian court determines that the chimpanzee Matthew does not have the same rights as a person.

2009 A European Union ban on animal testing for cosmetics goes into effect.

A lawsuit filed by ASPCA and other animal rights groups against Ringling Brothers and Barnum & Bailey Circus regarding the treatment of their elephants is heard in court.

GLOSSARY

anatomy: the study of the body

anesthesia: a chemical that renders a person or animal unconscious

anthropomorphism: the practice of assigning human traits to nonhuman animals or objects

carcinogenic: cancer causing

dominion: to have power over something or someone

endangered species: a species that is in danger of becoming extinct

euthanize: to kill in a painless way for reasons of mercy

extinction: the disappearance of a species

factory farm: large-scale, or intensive, farming

primate: a member of the order of mammals that includes human beings, monkeys, apes, and other related species

rational: having the ability to reason and understand

resolution: a formal statement of opinion or intent voted on by an official body or assembled group

sentient: to be aware of one's own consciousness and feelings

smallpox: a deadly disease that killed millions of people before a vaccine was developed

speciesism: the belief that human superiority justifies the use of other species for the benefits of humans

transgenic animal: an animal whose genetic code has been modified by adding a gene or genes from another species

vaccine: a medicine that is used to produce immunity to a certain disease

vegan: a person who does not eat animal products of any kind, including meat, eggs, milk, butter, or cheese

vegetarian: a person who does not eat the flesh of other animals

vivisection: the cutting open of a live animal to study its biological functions

SOURCE NOTES

6–7   Covance, "Animal Welfare Statement," *Covance*, n.d., http://www.covance
      .com/animalwelfare/index.php (January 22, 2009).

14   John Passmore, *Man's Responsibility for Nature* (New York: Scribner's, 1974), 6.

16   Mark Twain, "Mark Twain on Scientific Research," *Animals' Friend*, April
      1900, 99–100.

17   Richard Dudley Ryder, *Animal Revolution* (New York: Berg, 2000), 57.

18   Tom Regan, *The Case for Animal Rights*, 2nd ed. (Los Angeles: University of
      California Press, 2004), 177.

18–19 Ibid., 95.

20   Charles Darwin, *The Descent of Man, and Selection in Relation to Sex*
      (London: John Murray, Albemarle Street, 1890), 126

25   Peter Singer and Helga Kuhse, *Bioethics*, 2nd ed. (Malden, MA: Blackwell
      Publishing, 2006), 462.

26   Deborah Blum, *The Monkey Wars* (New York: Oxford University Press,
      1994), 142.

26   Dan Vergano, "Law Injected into Animal Testing; Researchers Cite Obstacles
      If Mice, Rats and Birds Are Protected," *USA TODAY*, October 31, 2000.

37   Animal Welfare Institute, "Humane Slaughter Act Resolution Introduced,"
      Animal Welfare Institute Quarterly, Summer 2001, http://www.awionline
      .org/pubs/Quarterly/summer2001/hsaintroduced.htm (January 22, 2009).

39   Humane Society of the United States, "Death of Approximately 150 Pigs
      in Texas Highlights USDA's Refusal to Implement Federal Humane Animal
      Transport Law," *Humane Society of the United States*, July 6, 2006, http://
      www.hsus.org/farm/news/pressrel/texas_pig_transportation.html
      (January 22, 2009).

46   Humane Society of the United States, "Students Slice through School
      Dissection Requirements," *Humane Society of the United States*, n.d., http://
      www.hsus.org/animals_in_research/animals_in_education/students_slice
      _through_school_dissection_requirements.html (January 22, 2009).

48   Ronald Bailey, "Kill the Vivisectors?" *Reason Online*, November 1, 2005,
      http://www.reason.com/blog/printer/111538.html (January 22, 2009).

49   U.S. Congress, "House Report 107–272," *U.S. Congress*, November 6, 2001,
      http://www.congress.gov/cgi-bin/cpquery/?&sid=cp107wxoo8&refer=&
      r_n=hr272.107&db_id=107&item=&sel=TOC_377316& (January 22, 2009).

49   Traci Watson, "Terror on the Beasts' Behalf," *USA TODAY*, November 12, 1998.

50   Jeffrey Stinson, "Activists Pursue Basic Legal Rights for Great Apes," *USA
      TODAY*, July 15, 2008.

51 Ed Yong, "Of Primates and Personhood," *Seed*, December 2009, 12.

54 Steve Sternberg, "Scientists Win Nobel for 'Designer Mice'; Altering Genes Opens Doors for Testing, Research," *USA TODAY*, October 9, 2007.

59 Erin Cassin, "AIDS Coalition Clashes with Animal Rights Activists," *New Standard*, September 20, 2005, http://newstandardnews.net/content/index .cfm/items/2378 (February 9, 2009).

65 John J. Pippin, "Replace Animal Experiments," *USA TODAY*, December 15, 2008.

70 Vergano, "Law Injected into Animal Testing."

71 *USA TODAY*, "High-Profile Cases of Cancer Place Spotlight on Research Methods," March 30, 2007.

80 Humane Farming Association, "About HFA," *Humane Farming Association*, n.d., http://www.hfa.org/about/index.html (January 22, 2009).

83 Animal Agricultural Alliance, "About the Alliance," *Animal Agricultural Alliance*, n.d., http://www.animalagalliance.org/current/home. cfm?Category=About_Us&Section=Main (January 22, 2009).

83 Elizabeth Weise, "PETA: 'Happy Cows' Ad Is a Lie; Group Plans Lawsuit Claiming Bovine Life Is Filthy, Inhumane," *USA TODAY*, December 11, 2002.

84 Jeff Tietz, "Bosshog," *Rolling Stone*, December 14, 2006, 89.

88 Mary Brophy Marcus, "Many Young People Go the Vegetarian Route; Choice Brings Concerns about Proper Nutrition," *USA TODAY*, October 15, 2007.

100 Dori Stehlin, "Cosmetic Safety: More Complex Than at First Blush," *FDA Consumer*, May 1995, http://www.cfsan.fda.gov/~dms/cos-safe.html (January 22, 2009).

114 Karen Dawn, *Thanking the Monkey: Rethinking the Way We Treat Animals* (New York: Harper, 2008), 63.

121 Martha Moore, "New Homes for Elephants Spur Debate," *USA TODAY*, June 3, 2005.

126 Dawn, *Thanking the Monkey*, 27.

132 State of Alaska, "Gov Issues Statement on ANWR Legislation," *State of Alaska*, January 14, 2009, http://www.gov.state.ak.us/news.php?id=1603 (January 22, 2009).

136 Larry Copeland, "Animal Rights Fight Gains Momentum," *USA TODAY*, January 28, 2008.

144 Yong, "Of Primates and Personhood," 12.

145 Constant Brand, "Goodall: Animal Testing Is 'Unacceptable,'" *USA TODAY*, May 28, 2008.

SELECTED BIBLIOGRAPHY

Beers, Diane L. *For the Prevention of Cruelty: The History and Legacy of Animal Rights Activism in the United States.* Athens, OH: Swallow Press / Ohio University Press, 2006.

Blum, Deborah. *The Monkey Wars.* New York: Oxford University Press, 1994.

Dawn, Karen. *Thanking the Monkey: Rethinking the Way We Treat Animals.* New York: Harper, 2008.

Fox, Michael. *Inhumane Society: The American Way of Exploiting Animals.* New York: St. Martin's Press, 1990.

Greek, Ray C., and Jean Swingle Greek. *Sacred Cows and Golden Geese: The Human Cost of Experiments on Animals.* New York: Continuum, 1990.

Kaufman, Les, and Kenneth Mallory. *The Last Extinction.* Cambridge: Massachusetts Institute of Technology Press, 1986.

Leader, Robert W., and Dennis Stark. *Animals in Biomedical Research.* Chicago: University of Chicago Press, 1987.

Passmore, John. *Man's Responsibility for Nature.* New York: Scribner's, 1974.

PETA Media Center. "Factsheets." *PETA.* N.d. http://www.peta.org/MC/facts.asp (January 26, 2009).

Regan, Tom. *The Case for Animal Rights.* 2nd ed. Los Angeles: University of California Press, 2004.

Rifkin, Jeremy. *Beyond Beef: The Rise and Fall of the Cattle Culture.* New York: Plume, 1993.

Rudacille, Deborah. *The Scalpel and the Butterfly: The War between Animal Research and Animal Protection.* New York: Farrar, Straus, and Giroux, 2000.

Sequoia, Anna. *67 Ways to Save the Animals.* New York: HarperCollins, 1990.

Singer, Peter. *Animal Liberation.* New York: Avon Books, 1975.

Singer, Peter, and Hekga Kuhse. *Bioethics*. 2nd ed. Malden, MA: Blackwell Publishing, 2006.

Wise, Steven M. *Rattling the Cage: Toward Legal Rights for Animals*. Cambridge, MA: Perseus Books, 2000.

ORGANIZATIONS TO CONTACT

The American Society for the Prevention of Cruelty to Animals (ASPCA)
424 E. 92nd Street
New York, NY 10128-6804
212-876-7700
http://www.aspca.org
The ASPCA is an animal welfare group devoted to ending animal cruelty. Its programs include animal welfare education, rescue and adoption programs, and spaying and neutering services for pets.

Animal Agriculture Alliance
P.O. Box 9522
Arlington, VA 22209
703-562-5160
http://www.animalagalliance.org
The Animal Agriculture Alliance is an organization of those involved in animal agriculture and the food industries to provide science-based education on the modern role of animal agriculture in the U.S. economy.

Foundation for Biomedical Research
818 Connecticut Avenue NW, Suite 900
Washington, DC 20006
202-457-0654
http://www.fbresearch.org
The Foundation for Biomedical Research is the United States' largest organization dedicated to improving human and veterinary health by promoting public understanding and support for humane and responsible animal research.

The Humane Farming Association
  P.O. Box 3577
  San Rafael, CA 94912
  415-771-2253
  http://www.hfa.org
  The Humane Farming Association's goals are to protect farm animals
  from cruelty; to protect the public from the dangerous misuse of
  antibiotics, hormones, and other chemicals used on factory farms; and
  to protect the environment from the impacts of industrialized animal
  factories.

The Humane Society of the United States
  2100 L Street NW
  Washington, DC 20037
  202-452-1100
  http://www.hsus.org
  The Humane Society of the United States is the nation's largest
  animal protection organization. It fights animal cruelty, exploitation,
  and neglect and promotes the positive bonds between humans and
  animals.

People for the Ethical Treatment of Animals (PETA)
  501 Front Street
  Norfolk, VA 23510
  757-622-7382
  http://www.peta.org
  PETA is an international organization that fights for animal rights
  through public education, investigation, legislation, and more.

U.S. Food and Drug Administration
  5600 Fishers Lane
  Rockville, MD 20857-0001
  888-463-6332
  http://www.fda.gov
  The FDA is the agency of the U.S. government responsible for the
  regulation and supervision of the safety of foods, drugs, medical
  products, and more.

FURTHER READING AND WEBSITES

Andryszewski, Tricia. *Mass Extinction: Examining the Current Crisis.* Minneapolis: Twenty-First Century Books, 2008.

The Animal Concerns Community
http://www.animalconcerns.org
This nonprofit organization provides access to thousands of animal rights resources, including news articles, legislation, and more.

Browning, Bel. *Animal Welfare.* Chicago: Raintree, 2003.

Currie-McGhee, L. K. *Animal Rights.* San Diego: Lucent Books, 2005.

Day, Nancy. *Animal Experimentation: Cruelty or Science?* Berkeley Heights, NJ: Enslow, 2000.

Fleisher, Paul. *Evolution.* Minneapolis: Twenty-First Century Books, 2006.

Friend, Catherine. *The Compassionate Carnivore: Or, How to Keep Animals Happy, Save Old Macdonald's Farm, Reduce Your Hoofprint, and Still Eat Meat.* Cambridge, MA: Da Capo Lifelong, 2008.

The Great Ape Project
http://www.greatapeproject.org
The Great Ape Project is an international group founded to fight for and protect the rights of the nonhuman great apes. The rights the project seeks include the right to life, the freedom of liberty, and protection from torture.

Judson, Karen. *Animal Testing.* New York: Marshall Cavendish Benchmark, 2006.

Miller, Deborah A., ed. *The Rights of Animals.* Detroit: Greenhaven Press, 2008.

Winkler, Kathleen. *Vegetarianism and Teens: A Hot Issue.* Springfield, NJ: Enslow, 2001.

INDEX

PHOTO ACKNOWLEDGMENTS

The images in this book are used with the permission of: © The Arizona Republic, August 17, 2005, Edythe Jensen/James Carreno. Used with permission. Permission does not imply endorsement, pp. 4–5; © iStockphoto.com/Bryan Myhr, p. 9; © A.A.M. Van der Heyden/Independent Picture Service, pp. 10–11; AP Photo/Rajesh Kumar Singh, p. 12; © Imagno/Hulton Archive/Getty Images, p. 15; The Granger Collection, New York, pp. 17, 18 (right); © Bildarchiv Preussischer Kulturbesitz/Art Resource, NY, p. 18 (left); Library of Congress, pp. 19 (LC-USZ62-52389), 36 (LC-DIG-ggbain-06185); © Michael Nichols/National Geographic/Getty Images, p. 22; © Alan Levenson/Time & Life Pictures/Getty Images, p. 23; AP Photo/Brian Branch-Price, p. 25; © Joe Raedle/ Newsmakers/Getty Images, p. 30; © Stockbyte/Getty Images, pp. 32–33; © RSPCA Photolibrary, p. 35; © Photononstop/SuperStock, p. 37; © Pascal Goetgheluck/Photo Researchers, Inc., pp. 42, 69; © Trinity Mirror/Mirrorpix/Alamy, p. 47; © Chris Holmes/ Time & Life Pictures/Getty Images, p. 48; AP Photo/Lilli Strauss, p. 50; © Robert Deutsch/USA TODAY, pp. 52–53; Centers for Disease Control and Prevention Public Health Image Library/Jean Roy, p. 54; © Popperfoto/Getty Images, p. 55; AP Photo/ Duane R. Miller, p. 57; AP Photo/Surgical Research Laboratories-Children's Hospital, p. 58; Animal Liberation Front, p. 61; Photo courtesy of PETA, p. 62; AP Photo/PA/Files, p. 67; © Dr. Jack Bostrack/Visuals Unlimited, Inc., p. 68; © Joshua Hatch/USA TODAY, pp. 72–73; © Robert Alan Benson/USA TODAY, p. 74; © Stephen Geffre/USA TODAY, p. 75; © Will & Deni McIntyre/Photo Researchers, Inc., p. 77; © Jewel Samad/AFP/ Getty Images, p. 79; Photo courtesy Farm Sanctuary, pp. 81, 82; AP Photo/Nati Harnik, pp. 85, 114; © P.C. Piazza/USA TODAY, p. 89; © National Trust Photographic Library/ Christopher Hurst/The Image Works, pp. 94–95; U.S. Food and Drug Administration, p. 97; © Siqui Sanchez/The Image Bank/Getty Images, p. 98; © Raveendran/AFP/Getty Images, p. 99; AP Photo/Mike Groll, p. 103; © Evan Eile/USA TODAY, p. 104; © Bettmann/CORBIS, p. 105; AP Photo/Bikas Das, p. 106; © Manny Ceneta/Getty Images, p. 107; AP Photo/Morry Gash, p. 109; © Chris Hondros/Getty Images, pp. 112–113, © Bill Luster, The Courier-Journal/USA TODAY, p. 116; © Bud Kraft, The Courier-Journal/USA TODAY, p. 117; © Ken Bohn/Zoological Society of San Diego/Getty Images, p. 119; AP Photo/Al Grillo, p. 120; © Robert Hanashiro/USA TODAY, p. 122; AP Photo/Jeff Roberson, p. 124; AP Photo/Texas A&M University, p. 125; AP Photo/Eric Gay, p. 127; © Johnny Johnson/The Image Bank/Getty Images, pp. 128–129; © Tim Dillon/ USA TODAY, pp. 138–139.

Front Cover: © Deco Images II/Alamy.

ABOUT THE AUTHOR

Marna Owen is a writer and instructional designer. After working as a juvenile hall counselor and probation officer in Alameda County, California, Ms. Owen began her writing career with a company specializing in high-interest materials for readers with special needs. Since then she has authored more than a dozen books for junior and senior high school students. She resides in Berkeley, California.